Martin Luther, Leonard Woolsey Bacon

Deutsche geistliche Lieder   the Hymns of Martin Luther

Set to their Original Melodies, with an English Version

Martin Luther, Leonard Woolsey Bacon

Deutsche geistliche Lieder   the Hymns of Martin Luther
Set to their Original Melodies, with an English Version

ISBN/EAN: 9783337127251

Printed in Europe, USA, Canada, Australia, Japan

Cover: Foto ©Thomas Meinert / pixelio.de

More available books at **www.hansebooks.com**

The Hymns of Luther.

Dr. Martin Luther's
Deutsche Geistliche Lieder

THE HYMNS OF
MARTIN LUTHER

SET TO THEIR ORIGINAL MELODIES

With an English Version

EDITED BY

LEONARD WOOLSEY BACON

ASSISTED BY

NATHAN H. ALLEN

New York

Published in Commemoration of the four hundredth Anniversary of
Luther's Birthday November 10 1483

By Charles Scribner's Sons

1883

CONTENTS.

FROM THE "EIGHT SONGS," Wittenberg, 1524.

"A song of Thanksgiving for the great Blessings which God in Christ has manifested to us."

DEAR CHRISTIANS, ONE AND ALL REJOICE.

TRANSLATION in part from R. Massie.

FIRST MELODY, 1524. Harmony by H. Schein, 1627.

SECOND MELODY from Klug's Gesangbuch, 1543. Harmony by M. Praetorius, 1610. This choral is commonly known under the title, "Es ist gewisslich an der Zeit," and, in a modified form, in England and America, as "Luther's Judgment Hymn," from its association with a hymn of W. B. Collyer, partly derived from the German, and *not* written by Luther.

PSALM XII—Salvum me fac, Domine.

LOOK DOWN, O LORD, FROM HEAVEN BEHOLD.

TRANSLATION chiefly from Frances Elizabeth Cox, in "Hymns from the German."

FIRST MELODY, 1524, is the tune of the hymn of Paul Speratus, "Es ist das Heil uns kommen her," the singing of which under Luther's window at Wittenberg is related to have made so deep an impression on the Reformer. The anecdote is confirmed by the fact that in the "Eight Songs," Luther's three versions of Psalms are all set to this tune. Harmony by A. Haupt, 1869.

SECOND MELODY from Klug's Gesangbuch, 1543. Harmony by Haupt, 1869. This is the tune in common use with this psalm in northern Germany.

CONTENTS.

FROM WALTER'S GESANGBUCH, 1525.

FROM THE GERMAN MASS, 1526.

IN "FORM UND ORDNUNG GEISTLICHER GESANG," Augsburg, 1529.

IN A COLLECTION OF "GEISTLICHE LIEDER," Wittenberg, 1533.

FROM JOSEPH KLUG'S GESANGSBUCH, 1535?

INTRODUCTION.

A FIT motto for the history of the Reformation would be those words out of the history of the Day of Pentecost, "How hear we, every man in our own tongue wherein we were born . . . . the wonderful works of God!" The ruling thought of the pre-reformation period was not more the maintenance of one Holy Roman Church than of one Holy Roman Empire, each of which was to comprehend all Christendom. The language of the Roman Church and Empire was the sacred language in comparison with which the languages of men's common speech were reckoned common and unclean. The coming-in of the Reformation was the awakening of individual life, by enforcing the sense of each man's direct responsibility to God; but it was equally the quickening of a true national life. In the light of the new era, the realization of the promise of the oneness of the Church was no longer to be sought in the universal dominance of a hierarchical corporation; nor was the "mystery" proclaimed by Paul, that "the nations were fellow-heirs and of one body," to be fulfilled in the subjugation of all nations to a central potentate. According to the spirit of the Reformation, the One Church was to be, not a corporation, but a communion—the communion of saints; and the unity of mankind, in its many nations, was to be a unity of the spirit in the bond of mutual peace.

The two great works of Martin Luther were those by which he gave to the common people a vernacular Bible and vernacular worship, that through the one, God might speak directly to the people; and in the other, the people might speak directly to God. Luther's Bible and Luther's Hymns gave life not only to the churches of the Reformation, but to German nationality and the German language.

Concerning the hymns of Luther the words of several notable writers are on record, and are worthy to be prefixed to the volume of them.

Says Spangenberg, yet in Luther's life-time, in his Preface to the *Cithara Lutheri,* 1545 :

"One must certainly let this be true, and remain true, that among all Master-singers from the days of the Apostles until now, Luther is and always will be the best and most accomplished ; in whose hymns and songs one does not find a vain or need-less word.   All flows and falls in the sweetest and neatest manner, full of spirit and doctrine, so that his every word gives outright a sermon of his own, or at least a sin-gular reminiscence.   There is nothing forced, nothing foisted in or patched up, noth-ing fragmentary.   The rhymes are easy and good, the words choice and proper, the meaning clear and intelligible, the melodies lovely and hearty, and *in summâ* all is so rare and majestic, so full of pith and power, so cheering and comforting, that, in sooth, you will not find his equal, much less his master." *

The following words have often been quoted from Samuel Taylor Cole-ridge :

"Luther did as much for the Reformation by his hymns as by his translation of the Bible.   In Germany the hymns are known by heart by every peasant ; they advise, they argue from the hymns, and every soul in the church praises God like a Christian, with words which are natural and yet sacred to his mind."

A striking passage in an article by Heine in the *Revue des Deux Mondes* for March, 1834, is transcribed by Michelet in his Life of Luther :

"Not less remarkable, not less significant than his prose works, are Luther's poems, those stirring songs which, as it were, escaped from him in the very midst of his combats and his necessities like a flower making its way from between rough stones, or a moonbeam gleaming amid dark clouds.   Luther loved music ; indeed, he wrote treatises on the art.   Accordingly his versification is highly harmonious, so that he may be called the Swan of Eisleben.   Not that he is by any means gentle or swan-like in the songs which he composed for the purpose of exciting the·courage of the people.   In these he is fervent, fierce.   The hymn which he composed on his way to Worms, and which he and his companions chanted as they entered that city,†

---

* Quoted in the *Christian Examiner,* 1860, p. 240 ; transcribed by the Rev. Bernhard Pick in "Luther as a Hymnist," p. 23 ; Philadelphia, 1875.

† The popular impression that the hymn " Ein' feste Burg " was produced in these circumstances is due, doubtless, to a parallel in the third stanza, to the famous saying imputed to Luther on the eve of the

is a regular war-song. The old cathedral trembled when it heard these novel sounds. The very rooks flew from their nests in the towers. That hymn, the Marseillaise of the Reformation, has preserved to this day its potent spell over German hearts."

The words of Thomas Carlyle are not less emphatic, while they penetrate deeper into the secret of the power of Luther's hymns:

"The great Reformer's love of music and poetry, it has often been remarked, is one of the most significant features in his character. But indeed if every great man is intrinsically a poet, an idealist, with more or less completeness of utterance, which of all our great men, in these modern ages, had such an endowment in that kind as Luther? He it was, emphatically, who stood based on the spiritual world of man, and only by the footing and power he had obtained there, could work such changes on the material world. As a participant and dispenser of divine influence, he shows himself among human affairs a true connecting medium and visible messenger between heaven and earth, a man, therefore, not only permitted to enter the sphere of poetry, but to dwell in the purest centre thereof, perhaps the most inspired of all teachers since the Apostles. Unhappily or happily, Luther's poetic feeling did not so much learn to express itself in fit words, that take captive every ear, as in fit actions, wherein, truly under still more impressive manifestations, the spirit of spheral melody resides and still audibly addresses us. In his written poems, we find little save that strength of one 'whose words,' it has been said, 'were half-battles' *— little of that still harmony and blending softness of union which is the last perfection of strength—less of it than even his conduct manifested. With words he had not learned to make music—it was by deeds of love or heroic valor that he spoke freely. Nevertheless, though in imperfect articulation, the same voice, if we listen well, is to be heard also in his writings, in his poems. The one entitled *Ein' Feste Burg*, universally regarded as the best, jars upon our ears; yet there is something in it like the sound of Alpine avalanches, or the first murmur of earthquakes, in the very vastness of which dissonance a higher unison is revealed to us. Luther wrote this song in times of blackest threatenings, which, however, could in no sense become a time of despair. In these tones, rugged and broken as they are, do we hear the accents of that summoned man, who answered his friends' warning not to enter Worms, in this wise:—'Were there as many devils in Worms as these tile

Diet of Worms: "I'll go, be there as many devils in the city as there be tiles on the roofs." The time of its composition was in the year 1529, just before the Diet of Augsburg. If not written in his temporary refuge, the noble "Burg" or "Festung" of Coburg, it must often have been sung there by him; and it was sung, says Merle d'Aubigné, "during the Diet, not only at Augsburg, but in all the churches of Saxony."

* This much-quoted phrase is from Richter. It is reported as an expression of Melanchthon, looking on Luther's picture, "*Fulmina erant singula verba tua.*"

roofs, I would on '; of him who, alone in that assemblage before all emperors and principalities and powers, spoke forth these final and forever memorable words,—' It is neither safe nor prudent to do aught against conscience. Till such time as either by proofs from holy Scripture, or by fair reason or argument, I have been confuted and convicted, I cannot and will not recant. Here I stand—I cannot do otherwise—God be my help, Amen.' It is evident enough that to this man all popes, cardinals, emperors, devils, all hosts and nations were but weak, weak as the forest with all its strong trees might be to the smallest spark of electric fire."

In a very different style of language, but in a like strain of eulogy, writes Dr. Merle d'Aubigné, in the third volume of his History of the Reformation :

"The church was no longer composed of priests and monks; it was now the congregation of believers. All were to take part in worship, and the chanting of the clergy was to be succeeded by the psalmody of the people. Luther, accordingly, in translating the psalms, thought of adapting them to be sung by the church. Thus a taste for music was diffused throughout the nation. From Luther's time, the people sang; the Bible inspired their songs. Poetry received the same impulse. In celebrating the praises of God, the people could not confine themselves to mere translations of ancient anthems. The souls of Luther and of several of his contemporaries, elevated by their faith to thoughts the most sublime, excited to enthusiasm by the struggles and dangers by which the church at its birth was unceasingly threatened, inspired by the poetic genius of the Old Testament and by the faith of the New, ere long gave vent to their feelings in hymns, in which all that is most heavenly in poetry and music was combined and blended. Hence the revival, in the sixteenth century, of *hymns*, such as in the first century used to cheer the martyrs in their sufferings. We have seen Luther, in 1523, employing it to celebrate the martyrs at Brussels; other children of the Reformation followed his footsteps; hymns were multiplied ; they spread rapidly among the people, and powerfully contributed to rouse it from sleep."

It is not difficult to come approximately at the order of composition of Luther's hymns. The earliest hymn-book of the Reformation—if not the earliest of all printed hymn-books—was published at Wittenberg in 1524, and contained *eight* hymns, four of them from the pen of Luther himself; of the other four not less than three were by Paul Speratus, and one of these three, the hymn *Es ist das Heil*, which caused Luther such delight when sung beneath his window by a wanderer from Prussia.* Three of Luther's con-

---

* Merle d'Aubigné, History of the Reformation, Vol. III.

tributions to this little book were versions of Psalms—the xii, xiv, and cxxx —and the fourth was that touching utterance of personal religious experience, *Nun freut euch, lieben Christen g'mein.* But the critics can hardly be mistaken in assigning as early a date to the ballad of the Martyrs of Brussels. Their martyrdom took place July 1, 1523, and the "*New Song*" must have been inspired by the story as it was first brought to Wittenberg, although it is not found in print until the *Enchiridion*, which followed the *Eight Hymns*, later in the same year, from the press of Erfurt, and contained fourteen of Luther's hymns beside the four already published.

In the hymn-book published in 1525 by the composer Walter, Luther's friend, were six more of the Luther hymns. And in 1526 appeared the "German Mass and Order of Divine Service," containing "the German Sanctus," a versification of Isaiah vi. Of the remaining eleven, six appeared first in the successive editions of Joseph Klug's hymn-book, Wittenberg, 1535 and 1543.

It is appropriate to the commemorative character of the present edition that in it the hymns should be disposed in chronological order.

The TUNES which are here printed with the hymns of Luther are of those which were set to them during his lifetime. Some of them, like the hymns to which they were set, are derived from the more ancient hymnody of the German and Latin churches. Others, as the tunes *Vom Himmel hoch, Ach Gott vom Himmel,* and *Christ unser Herr zum Jordan kam,* are conjectured to have been originally secular airs. But that many of the tunes that appeared simultaneously and in connection with Luther's hymns were original with Luther himself, there seems no good reason to doubt. Luther's singular delight and proficiency in music are certified by a hundred contemporary testimonies. His enthusiasm for it overflows in his Letters and his Table Talk. He loved to surround himself with accomplished musicians, with whom he would practise the intricate motets of the masters of that age; and his critical remarks on their several styles are on record. At least one autograph document proves him to have been a composer of melodies to his own words: one may see, appended to von Winterfeld's fine quarto edition of Luther's hymns (Leipzig, 1840) a fac-simile of the original draft of *Vater Unser,* with a melody sketched upon a staff of five lines, and then cancelled, evidently by a hand practised in musical notation. But perhaps the most direct testimony to his actual work as a composer is found in a letter from the composer John Walter, capellmeister to the Elector of Saxony, written in his old age for the express purpose of embodying his reminiscences of his illustrious friend as a church-musician.

"It is to my certain knowledge," writes Walter, "that that holy man of God, Luther, prophet and apostle to the German nation, took great delight in music, both in choral and in figural composition. With whom I have passed many a delightful hour in singing; and oftentimes have seen the dear man wax so happy and merry in heart over the singing as that it was well-nigh impossible to weary or content him therewithal. And his discourse concerning music was most noble.

"Some forty years ago, when he would set up the German Mass at Wittenberg, he wrote to the Elector of Saxony and Duke Johannsen, of illustrious memory, begging to invite to Wittenberg the old musician Conrad Rupff and myself, to consult with him as to the character and the proper notation of the Eight Tones; and he finally himself decided to appropriate the Eighth Tone to the Epistle and the Sixth Tone to the Gospel, speaking on this wise: Our Lord Christ is a good Friend, and his words are full of love; so we will take the Sixth Tone for the Gospel. And since Saint Paul is a very earnest apostle we will set the Eighth Tone to the Epistle. So he himself made the notes over the Epistles, and the Gospels, and the Words of Institution of the true Body and Blood of Christ, and sung them over to me to get my judgment thereon. He kept me three weeks long at Wittenberg, to write out the notes over some of the Gospels and Epistles, until the first German Mass was sung in the parish church. And I must needs stay to hear it, and take with me a copy of the Mass to Torgau and present it to His Grace the Elector from Doctor Luther.

"Furthermore, he gave orders to re-establish the Vespers, which in many places were fallen into disuse, with short plain choral hymns for the students and boys; withal, that the charity-scholars, collecting their bread, should sing from door to door Latin Hymns, Anthems and Responses, appropriate to the season. It was no satisfaction to him that the scholars should sing in the streets nothing but German songs. . . . The most profitable songs for the common multitude are the plain psalms and hymns, both Luther's and the earlier ones; but the Latin songs are useful for the learned and for students. We see, and hear, and clearly apprehend how the Holy Ghost himself wrought not only in the authors of the Latin hymns, but also in Luther, who in our time has had the chief part both in writing the German choral hymns, and in setting them to tunes; as may be seen, among others in the German Sanctus (*Jesaia dem Propheten das geschah*) how masterly and well he has fitted all the notes to the text, according to the just accent and concent. At the time, I was moved by His Grace to put the question how or where he had got

this composition, or this instruction ; whereupon the dear man laughed at my sim-
plicity, and said : I learned this of the poet Virgil, who has the power so artfully to
adapt his verses and his words to the story he is telling ; in like manner must Music
govern all its notes and melodies by the text." *

It seems superfluous to add to this testimony the word of Sleidan, the
nearly contemporary historian, who says expressly concerning "*Ein' feste
Burg*" that Luther made for it a tune singularly suited to the words, and
adapted to stir the heart.† If ever there were hymn and tune that told their
own story of a common and simultaneous origin, without need of confirma-
tion by external evidence, it is these.

To an extent quite without parallel in the history of music, the power
of Luther's tunes, as well as of his words, is manifest after three centuries,
over the masters of the art, as well as over the common people. Peculiarly
is this true of the great song *Ein' feste Burg*, which Heine not vainly pre-
dicted would again be heard in Europe in like manner as of old. The com-
posers of the sixteenth and seventeenth centuries practised their elaborate
artifices upon it. The supreme genius of Sebastian Bach made it the sub-
ject of study.‡ And in our own times it has been used with conspicuous
effect in Mendelssohn's Reformation Symphony, in an overture by Raff, in
the noble *Festouverture* of Nicolai, and in Wagner's Kaisermarsch ; and is
introduced with recurring emphasis in Meyerbeer's masterpiece of The
Huguenots.

It is needless to say that the materials of this Birth-day Edition of
Luther's Hymns and Tunes have been prepared in profusion by the diligence
of German scholars. But very thankful acknowledgments are also due to
English translators, who have made this work possible within the very
scanty time allotted to it. Full credit is given in the table of contents for
the help derived from these various translators. But the exigencies of this

---

* This interesting and characteristic document was printed first in the *Syntagma Musicum* of Michael
Praetorius, many of whose harmonies are to be found in this volume. It has been repeatedly copied since.
I take it from Rambach, " Ueber D. Martin Luthers Verdienst um den Kirchengesang, oder Darstellung
desjenigen was er als Liturg, als Liederdichter und Tonsetzer zur Verbesserung des öffentlichen Gottes-
dienstes geleistet hat. Hamburg, 1813."

† Quoted in Rambach, p. 215.

‡ In more than one of his cantatas, especially that for the Reformationsfest.

volume were peculiarly severe, inasmuch as the translation was to be printed over against the original, and also under the music. Not even Mr. Richard Massie's careful work would always bear this double test; so that I have found myself compelled, in most cases, to give up the attempt to follow any translation exactly; and in some instances have reluctantly attempted a wholly new version.

The whole credit of the musical editorship belongs to my accomplished associate, Mr. Nathan H. Allen, without whose ready resource and earnest labor the work would have been impossible within the limits of time necessarily prescribed. In the choice of harmonies for these ancient tunes, he has wisely preferred, in general, the arrangements of the older masters. The critical musician will see, and will not complain, that the original modal structure of the melodies is sometimes affected by the harmonic treatment.

And now the proper conclusion to this Introduction, which, like the rest of the volume, is in so slight a degree the work of the editor, is to add the successive prefaces from the pen of Luther which accompanied successive hymn-books published during his life-time and under his supervision.

LEONARD WOOLSEY BACON.

Luther's First Preface.

To the „Geyſtliche Gſangbüchlin, Erſtlich zu Wittenberg, und volgend durch Peter ſchöffern getruckt, im jar m. d. xxv.
Autore IOANNE WALTHERO."

THAT it is good, and pleasing to God, for us to sing spiritual songs is, I think, a truth whereof no Christian can be ignorant; since not only the example of the prophets and kings of the Old Testament (who praised God with singing and music, poesy and all kinds of stringed instruments) but also the like practice of all Christendom from the beginning, especially in respect to psalms, is well known to every one: yea, St. Paul doth also appoint the same (1 Cor xiv.) and command the Colossians, in the third chapter, to sing spiritual songs and psalms from the heart unto the Lord, that thereby the word of God and Christian doctrine be in every way furthered and practised.

Accordingly, to make a good beginning and to encourage others who can do it better, I have myself, with some others, put together a few hymns, in order to bring into full play the blessed Gospel, which by God's grace hath again risen: that we may boast, as Moses doth in his song (Exodus xv.) that Christ is become our praise and our song, and that, whether we sing or speak, we may not know anything save Christ our Saviour, as St. Paul saith (1 Cor. ii.).

These songs have been set in four parts, for no other reason than because I wished to provide our young people (who both will and ought to be instructed in music and other sciences) with something whereby they might rid themselves of amorous and carnal songs, and in their stead learn something wholesome, and so apply themselves to what is good with pleasure, as becometh the young.

Beside this, I am not of opinion that all sciences should be beaten down and made to cease by the Gospel, as some fanatics pretend; but I would fain see all the arts, and music in particular, used in the service of Him who hath given and created them.

Therefore I entreat every pious Christian to give a favorable reception to these hymns, and to help forward my undertaking, according as God hath given him more or less ability. The world is, alas, not so mindful and diligent to train and teach our poor youth, but that we ought to be forward in promoting the same. God grant us his grace. Amen.

Luther's Second Preface.

To the Funeral Hymns: „Chriſtliche Geſeng, Lateiniſch und Deudſch, zum Begrebnis. Wittemberg, Anno m. d. xlii.“

DR. MARTIN LUTHER TO THE CHRISTIAN READER.

ST. PAUL writes to the Thessalonians, that they should not sorrow for the dead as others who have no hope, but should comfort one another with God's word, as they who have a sure hope of life and of the resurrection of the dead.

For that they should sorrow who have no hope is not to be wondered at, nor indeed are they to be blamed for it, since, being shut out from the faith of Christ, they must either regard and love the present life only, and be loth to lose it, or after this life look for everlasting death and the wrath of God in hell, and be unwilling to go thither.

But we Christians who from all this have been redeemed by the precious blood of the Son of God, should exercise and wont ourselves in faith to despise death, to look on it as a deep, sound, sweet sleep, the coffin no other than the bosom of our Lord Christ, or paradise, the grave nought but a soft couch of rest; as indeed it is in the sight of God, as he saith in St. John, xi., "our friend Lazarus sleepeth;" Matthew ix., "the maid is not dead but sleepeth."

In like manner also St. Paul, 1 Cor. xv., doth put out of sight the unlovely aspect of death in our perishing body, and bring forward nought but the lovely and delightsome view of life, when he saith : "It is sown in corruption; it is raised in incorruption; it is sown in dishonor (that is, in a loathsome and vile form); it is raised in glory : it is sown in weakness; it is raised in power: it is sown a natural body ; it is raised a spiritual body."

Accordingly have we, in our churches, abolished, done away, and out-and-out made an end of the popish horrors, such as wakes, masses for the soul, obsequies, purgatory, and all other mummeries for the dead, and will no longer have our churches turned into wailing-places and houses of mourning, but, as the primitive Fathers called them, "Cemeteries," that is, resting and sleeping places.

We sing, withal, beside our dead and over their graves, no dirges nor lamentations, but comforting songs of the forgiveness of sins, of rest, sleep, life and resurrection of the departed believers, for the strengthening of our faith, and the stirring up of the people to a true devotion.

For it is meet and right to give care and honor to the burial of the dead, in a manner worthy of that blessed article of our creed, the resurrection of the dead, and to the spite of that dreadful enemy, death, who doth so shamefully and continually prey upon us, in every horrid way and shape.

Accordingly, as we read, the holy patriarchs, Abraham, Isaac, Jacob, Joseph, and the rest, kept their burials with great pomp, and ordered them with much diligence ; and afterwards the kings of Judah held splendid ceremonials over the dead, with costly incense of all manner of precious herbs, thereby to hide the offense and shame of death, and acknowledge and glorify the resurrection of the dead, and so to comfort the weak in faith and the sorrowful.

In like manner, even down to this present, have Christians ever been wont to do honorably by the bodies and the graves of the dead, decorating them, singing beside them and adorning them with monuments. Of all importance is that doctrine of the resurrection, that we be firmly grounded therein ; for it is our lasting, blessed, eternal comfort and joy, against death, hell, the devil and all sorrow of heart.

As a good example of what should be used for this end, we have taken the sweet music or melodies which under popish rule are in use at wakes, funerals and masses for the dead, some of which we have printed in this little book ; and it is in our thought, as time shall serve, to add others to them, or have this done by more competent hands. But we have set other words thereto, such as shall adorn our doctrine of the resurrection, not that of purgatory with its pains and expiations, whereby the dead may neither sleep nor rest. The notes and melodies are of great price ; it were pity to let them perish : but the words to them were unchristian and uncouth, so let these perish.

It is just as in other matters they do greatly excel us, having splendid rites of worship, magnificent convents and abbeys ; but the preachings and doctrines heard therein do for the most part serve the devil and dishonor God ; who nevertheless is Lord and God over all the earth, and should have of everything the fairest, best and noblest.

Likewise have they costly shrines of gold and silver, and images set with gems and jewels ; but within are dead men's bones, as foul and corrupt as in any charnel-house. So also have they costly vestments, chasubles, palliums, copes, hoods, mitres, but what are they that be clothed therewithal? slow-bellies, evil wolves, godless swine, persecuting and dishonoring the word of God.

Just in the same way have they much noble music, especially in the abbeys and parish churches, used to adorn most vile, idolatrous words. Wherefore we have undressed these idolatrous, lifeless, crazy words, stripping off the noble music, and putting it upon the living and holy word of God, wherewith to sing, praise and honor the same, that so the beautiful ornament of music, brought back to its right use, may serve its blessed Maker and his Christian people ; so that he shall be praised and glorified, and that we by his holy word impressed upon the heart with sweet songs, be builded up and confirmed in the faith. Hereunto help us God the Father, Son and Holy Ghost. Amen.

Yet is it not our purpose that these precise notes be sung in all the churches. Let each church keep its own notes according to its book and use. For I myself do not listen with pleasure in cases where the notes to a hymn or a *responsorium* have been changed, and it is sung amongst us in a different way from what I have been used to from my youth. The main point is the correcting of the words, not of the music.

[Then follow selections of Scripture recommended as suitable for epitaphs.]

Luther's Third Preface.

To the Hymn-book printed at Wittenberg by Joseph Klug, 1543.

THERE are certain who, by their additions to our hymns, have clearly shown that they far excel me in this matter, and may well be called my masters. But some, on the other hand, have added little of value. And inasmuch as I see that there is no limit to this perpetual amending by every one indiscriminately according to his own liking, so that the earliest of our hymns are more perverted the more they are printed, I am fearful that it will fare with this little book as it has ever fared with good books, that through tampering by incompetent hands it may get to be so overlaid and spoiled that the good will be lost out of it, and nothing be kept in use but the worthless.

We see in the first chapter of St. Luke that in the beginning every one wanted to write a gospel, until among the multitude of gospels the true Gospel was well-nigh lost. So has it been with the works of St. Jerome and St. Augustine, and with many other books. In short, there will always be tares sown among the wheat.

In order as far as may be to avoid this evil, I have once more revised this book, and put our own hymns in order by themselves with name attached, which formerly I would not do for reputation's sake, but am now constrained to do by necessity, lest strange and unsuitable songs come to be sold under our name. After these, are arranged the others, such as we deem good and useful.

I beg and beseech all who prize God's pure word that henceforth without our knowledge and consent no further additions or alterations be made in this book of ours; and that when it is amended without our knowledge, it be fully understood to be not our book published at Wittenberg. Every man can for himself make his own hymn-book, and leave this of ours alone without additions; as we here beg, beseech and testify. For we like to keep our coin up to our own standard, debarring no man from making better for himself. Now let God's name alone be praised, and our name not sought. Amen.

Luther's Fourth Preface.

To Valentine Bapst's Hymn-book, Leipzig, 1545.

THE xcvi Psalm saith : " Sing to the Lord a new song ; sing to the Lord, all the earth." The service of God in the old dispensation, under the law of Moses, was hard and wearisome. Many and divers sacrifices had men to offer, of all that they possessed, both in house and in field, which the people, being idle and covetous, did grudgingly or for some temporal advantage ; as the prophet Malachi saith, chap. i., " who is there even among you that would shut the doors for naught ? neither do ye kindle fires on my altars for naught." But where there is such an idle and grudging heart there can be no singing, or at least no singing of anything good. Cheerful and merry must we be in heart and mind, when we would sing. Therefore hath God suffered such idle and grudging service to perish, as he saith further : " I have no pleasure in you, saith the Lord of Hosts, neither will I accept an offering at your hand : for from the rising of the sun even to the going down of the same, my name shall be great among the Gentiles ; and in every place incense shall be offered in my name and a pure offering ; for my name shall be great among the heathen, saith the Lord of Hosts."

So that now in the New Testament there is a better service, whereof the psalm speaketh : " Sing to the Lord a new song ; sing to the Lord all the earth." For God hath made our heart and mind joyful through his dear Son whom he hath given for us to redeem us from sin, death and the devil. Who earnestly believes this cannot but sing and speak thereof with joy and delight, that others also may hear and come. But whoso will not speak and sing thereof, it is a sign that he doth not believe it, and doth not belong to the cheerful New Testament but to the dull and joyless Old Testament.

Therefore it is well done on the part of the printers that they are diligent to print good hymns, and make them agreeable to the people with all sorts of embellishments, that they may be won to this joy in believing and gladly sing of it. And inasmuch as this edition of Valtin Bapst [Pope] is prepared in fine style, God grant that it may bring great hurt and damage to that Roman *Bapst* who by his accursed, intolerable and abominable ordinances has brought nothing into the world but wailing, mourning and misery. Amen.

I must give notice that the song which is sung at funerals,

"Nun lasst uns den Leib begraben,"

which bears my name is not mine, and my name is henceforth not to stand with it. Not that I reject it, for I like it very much, and it was made by a good poet, Johannes Weis * by name, only a little visionary about the Sacrament ; but I will not appropriate to myself another man's work.

Also in the *De Profundis*, read thus:

Des muss *dich* fürchten jedermann.

Either by mistake or of purpose this is printed in most books

Des muss *sich* fürchten jedermann.

Ut timearis. The Hebrew reading is as in Matthew xv. : " In vain do they fear me teaching doctrines of men." See also Psalms xiv. and liii. : " They call not on the Lord ; there feared they where no fear was." That is, they may have much show of humiliation and bowing and bending in worship where I will have no worship. Accordingly this is the meaning in this place : Since forgiveness of sins is nowhere else to be found but only with thee, so must they let go all idolatry, and come with a willing heart bowing and bending before thee, creeping up to the cross, and have thee alone in honor, and take refuge in thee, and serve thee, as living by thy grace and not by their own righteousness, etc.

* Luther's mistake for *Michael Weysse,* author of a Moravian hymn-book of 1531.

A Preface to All Good Hymn-Books.

By Dr. Martin Luther.

From Joseph Klug's Hymn-Book, Wittenberg, 1543.

Lady Musick Speaketh.

Of all the joys that are on earth
Is none more dear nor higher worth,
Than what in my sweet songs is found
And instruments of various sound.

Where friends and comrades sing in tune,
All evil passions vanish soon ;
Hate, anger, envy, cannot stay,
All gloom and heartache melt away ;
The lust of wealth, the cares that cling,
Are all forgotten while we sing.

Freely we take our joy herein,
For this sweet pleasure is no sin,
But pleaseth God far more, we know,
Than any joys the world can show ;
The Devil's work it doth impede,
And hinders many a deadly deed.

So fared it with King Saul of old ;
When David struck his harp of gold,
So sweet and clear its tones rang out,
Saul's murderous thoughts were put to rout.

The heart grows still when I am heard,
And opens to God's Truth and Word;
So are we by Elisha taught,
Who on the harp the Spirit sought.

The best time of the year is mine,
When all the little birds combine
To sing until the earth and air
Are filled with sweet sounds everywhere ;
And most the tender nightingale
Makes joyful every wood and dale,
Singing her love-song o'er and o'er,
For which we thank her evermore.

But yet more thanks are due from us
To the dear Lord who made her thus,
A singer apt to touch the heart,
Mistress of all my dearest art.
To God she sings by night and day,
Unwearied, praising Him alway ;
Him I, too, laud in every song,
To whom all thanks and praise belong.

Translation by
CATHARINE WINKWORTH.

A Warning by Dr. Martin Luther.

Viel falscher Meister itzt Lieder tichten
Sihe dich fuer vnd lern sie recht richten
Wo Gott hin bawet sein Kirch vnd sein wort
Da will der Teufel sein mit trug vnd mord.
Wittenberg, 1543; Leipzig, 1545.

False masters now abound, who songs indite ;
Beware of them, and learn to judge them right :
Where God builds up his Church and Word, hard by
Satan is found with murder and a lie.

Translation by R. MASSIE.

I. Nun freut euch, lieben Christen g'mein.

Dear Christians, One and All rejoice.

A Song of Thanksgiving for the great Benefits which God in Christ has manifested to us.

FIRST MELODY, *Wittenberg*, 1524.　　　　　　　　　*Harmony by* H. SCHEIN, 1627.

{ Dear Christians, one and all re - joice, With ex - ul - ta-tion spring-ing, }
{ And with u - nit - ed heart and voice And ho - ly rap-ture sing - ing, }　Pro-claim the

won-ders God hath done, How his right arm the vic - t'ry won; Right dear-ly it hath cost　him.

SECOND MELODY, *Wittenberg*, 1535.　　　　　　　　*Harmony by* M. PRAETORIUS, 1610.

{ Dear Christians, one and all re - joice, With ex - ul - ta -tion spring　-　ing, }
{ And with u - nit - ed heart and voice And ho - ly rap-ture sing　-　ing, }　Pro-claim the

wonders God hath done, How his right arm the vic - t'ry won ; Right dear - ly　it hath cost　him.

Nun freut euch, lieben Christen g'mein.

Dear Christians, One and All rejoice.

1 Nun freut euch, lieben Christen g'mein,
   Und laßt uns fröhlich springen,
   Daß wir getrost und all in ein
   Mit Lust und Liebe singen:
   Was Gott an uns gewendet hat,
   Und seine süße Wunderthat,
   Gar theur hat er's erworben.

2 Dem Teufel ich gefangen lag,
   Im Tod war ich verloren,
   Mein' Sünd' mich quälet Nacht und Tag,
   Darin war ich geboren,
   Ich fiel auch immer tiefer d'rein,
   Es war kein gut's am Leben mein,
   Die Sünd' hat mich besessen.

3 Mein' gute Werk' die galten nicht,
   Es war mit ihm verdorben;
   Der frei Will' hasset Gottes G'richt,
   Er war zum Gut'n erstorben;
   Die Angst mich zu verzweifeln trieb,
   Daß nichts denn Sterben bei mir blieb,
   Zur Hölle mußt ich sinken.

4 Da jammert's Gott in Ewigkeit
   Mein Elend über Maßen,
   Er dacht' an sein' Barmherzigkeit,
   Er wollt' mir helfen lassen;
   Er wandt' zu mir das Vaterherz,
   Es war bei ihm fürwahr kein Scherz,
   Er ließ sein Bestes kosten.

5 Er sprach zu seinem lieben Sohn:
   Die Zeit ist hier zu 'rbarmen,
   Fahr' hin mein's Herzens werthe Kron'
   Und sei das Heil dem Armen,
   Und hilf ihm aus der Sünden Noth,
   Erwürg' für ihn den bittern Tod
   Und laß' ihn mit dir leben.

1 Dear Christians, one and all rejoice,
   With exultation springing,
   And with united heart and voice
   And holy rapture singing, ·
   Proclaim the wonders God hath done,
   How his right arm the victory won ;
   Right dearly it hath cost him.

2 Fast bound in Satan's chains I lay,
   Death brooded darkly o'er me ;
   Sin was my torment night and day,
   Therein my mother bore me.
   Deeper and deeper still I fell,
   Life was become a living hell,
   So firmly sin possessed me.

3 My good works could avail me naught,
   For they with sin were stainéd ;
   Free-will against God's judgment fought,
   And dead to good remainéd.
   Grief drove me to despair, and I
   Had nothing left me but to die,
   To hell I fast was sinking.

4 God saw, in his eternal grace,
   My sorrow out of measure ;
   He thought upon his tenderness—
   To save was his good pleasure.
   He turn'd to me a Father's heart-
   Not small the cost—to heal my smart
   He gave his best and dearest.

5 He spake to his beloved Son :
   'Tis time to take compassion ;
   Then go, bright jewel of my crown,
   And bring to man salvation ;
   From sin and sorrow set him free,
   Slay bitter death for him, that he
   May live with thee forever.

FIRST MELODY, *Wittenberg*, 1524.   *Harmony by* H. SCHEIN, 1627.

{ Dear Christians, one and all re - joice, With ex - ul - ta - tion spring - ing, }
{ And with u - nit - ed heart and voice And ho - ly rap-ture sing - ing, }   Pro-claim the

won-ders God hath done, How his right arm the vic - t'ry won; Right dear- ly it hath cost   him.

SECOND MELODY, *Wittenberg*, 1535.   *Harmony by* M. PRAETORIUS, 1610.

{ Dear Christians, one and all re - joice, With ex - ul - ta - tion spring - ing, }
{ And with u - nit - ed heart and voice And ho - ly rap-ture sing - ing, }   Pro-claim the

wonders God hath done, How his right arm the vic - t'ry won ; Right dear - ly it hath cost   him.

6 Der Sohn dem Vater g'horsam ward,
  Er kam zu mir auf Erden,
  Von einer Jungfrau rein und zart,
  Er sollt' mein Bruder werden.
  Gar heimlich führt er sein' Gewalt,
  Er ging in meiner armen G'stalt,
  Den Teufel wollt' er fangen.

6 The Son delighted to obey,
  And born of Virgin mother,
  Awhile on this low earth did stay
  That he might be my brother.
  His mighty power he hidden bore,
  A servant's form like mine he wore,
  To bind the devil captive.

7 Er sprach zu mir: halt' dich an mich,
  Es soll dir jetzt gelingen,
  Ich geb' mich selber ganz für dich,
  Da will ich für dich ringen;
  Denn ich bin dein und du bist mein,
  Und wo ich bleib', da sollst du sein,
  Uns soll der Feind nicht scheiden.

7 To me he spake : cling fast to me,
  Thou'lt win a triumph worthy ;
  I wholly give myself for thee,
  I strive and wrestle for thee ;
  For I am thine, thou mine also ;
  And where I am thou art. The foe
  Shall never more divide us.

8 Vergießen wird er mir mein Blut,
  Dazu mein Leben rauben,
  Das leid' ich alles dir zu gut,
  Das halt' mit festem Glauben.
  Den Tod verschlingt das Leben mein,
  Mein' Unschuld trägt die Sünde dein,
  Da bist du selig worden.

8 For he shall shed my precious blood,
  Me of my life bereaving ;
  All this I suffer for thy good ;
  Be steadfast and believing.
  My life from death the day shall win,
  My righteousness shall bear thy sin,
  So art thou blest forever.

9 Gen Himmel zu dem Vater mein
  Fahr' ich von diesem Leben,
  Da will ich sein der Meister dein,
  Den Geist will ich dir geben,
  Der dich in Trübniß trösten soll
  Und lehren mich erkennen wohl,
  Und in der Wahrheit leiten.

9 Now to my Father I depart,
  From earth to heaven ascending ;
  Thence heavenly wisdom to impart,
  The Holy Spirit sending.
  He shall in trouble comfort thee,
  Teach thee to know and follow me,
  And to the truth conduct thee.

10 Was ich gethan hab' und gelehrt,
  Das sollst du thun und lehren,
  Damit das Reich Gott's werd' gemehrt
  Zu Lob' und seinen Ehren;
  Und hüt' dich vor der Menschen G'satz,
  Davon verdirbt der edle Schatz,
  Das laß' ich dir zur Letze.

10 What I have done and taught, do thou
  To do and teach endeavor ;
  So shall my kingdom flourish now,
  And God be praised forever.
  Take heed lest men with base alloy
  The heavenly treasure should destroy.
  This counsel I bequeath thee.

11. Ach Gott, vom Himmel sieh' darein.

Look down, O Lord, from Heaven behold.

PSALM XII.—"*Salvum me fac, Domine.*"

FIRST MELODY, *Wittenberg*, 1524. *Harmony by* A. HAUPT, 1869.

{ Look down, O Lord, from heav'n be - hold, And let thy pit - y wak - en! }
{ How few the flock with - in thy fold, Neg-lect-ed and for - sak - en! } Almost thou'lt seek for

faith in vain, And those who should thy truth main-tain Thy Word from us have tak - en.

SECOND MELODY, *Wittenberg*, 1543. *Harmony by* A. HAUPT, 1869.

{ Look down, O Lord, from heav'n behold, And let thy pit - y wak - en! }
{ How few the flock with - in thy fold, Neg-lect-ed and for - sak - en! } Almost thou'lt seek for

faith in vain, And those who should thy truth main-tain Thy Word from us have tak - en.

Ach Gott, vom Himmel sieh' darein.

Look down, O Lord, from Heaven behold.

1 Ach Gott, vom Himmel sieh' darein
Und laß' dich des erbarmen,
Wie wenig sind der Heil'gen dein,
Verlassen sind wir Armen:
Dein Wort man läßt nicht haben wahr,
Der Glaub' ist auch verloschen gar
Bei allen Menschenkindern.

2 Sie lehren eitel falsche List,
Was eigen Witz erfindet,
Ihr Herz nicht eines Sinnes ist
In Gottes Wort gegründet;
Der wählet dies, der Ander das,
Sie trennen uns ohn' alle Maas
Und gleißen schön von außen.

3 Gott woll' ausrotten alle Lahr,
Die falschen Schein uns lehren;
Dazu ihr' Zung' stolz offenbar
Spricht: Trotz, wer will's uns wehren?
Wir haben Recht und Macht allein,
Was wir setzen das gilt gemein,
Wer ist der uns soll meistern?

4 Darum spricht Gott, Ich muß auf sein,
Die Armen sind verstöret,
Ihr Seufzen dringt zu mir herein,
Ich hab' ihr' Klag' erhöret.
Mein heilsam Wort soll auf dem Plan,
Getrost und frisch sie greifen an
Und sein die Kraft der Armen.

5 Das Silber durch's Feuer siebenmal
Bewährt, wird lauter funden:
Am Gottes Wort man warten soll
Desgleichen alle Stunden:
Es will durch's Kreuz bewähret sein,
Da wird sein' Kraft erkannt und Schein
Und leucht't stark in die Lande.

6 Das wollst du, Gott, bewahren rein
Für diesem argen G'schlechte,
Und laß uns dir befohlen sein,
Das sich's in uns nicht flechte,
Der gottlos' Hauf' sich umher findt,
Wo diese lose Leute sind
In deinem Volk erhaben.

1 Look down, O Lord, from heaven behold,
And let thy pity waken!
How few the flock within thy fold,
Neglected and forsaken!
Almost thou'lt seek for faith in vain,
And those who should thy truth maintain
Thy Word from us have taken.

2 With frauds which they themselves invent
Thy truth they have confounded;
Their hearts are not with one consent
On thy pure doctrine grounded;
And, whilst they gleam with outward show,
They lead thy people to and fro,
In error's maze astounded.

3 God surely will uproot all those
With vain deceits who store us,
With haughty tongue who God oppose,
And say, "Who'll stand before us?
By right or might we will prevail;
What we determine cannot fail,
For who can lord it o'er us?"

4 For this, saith God, I will arise,
These wolves my flock are rending;
I've heard my people's bitter sighs
To heaven my throne ascending:
Now will I up, and set at rest
Each weary soul by fraud opprest,
The poor with might defending.

5 The silver seven times tried is pure
From all adulteration;
So, through God's word, shall men endure
Each trial and temptation:
Its worth gleams brighter through the cross,
And, purified from human dross,
It shines through every nation.

6 Thy truth thou wilt preserve, O Lord,
From this vile generation;
Make us to lean upon thy word,
With calm anticipation.
The wicked walk on every side
When, 'mid thy flock, the vile abide
In power and exaltation.

111. Es spricht der Unweisen Mund wohl.

The Mouth of Fools doth God confess.

PSALM XIV. — "*Dixit insipiens in corde suo, Non est Deus.*"

MELODY, *Wittenberg*, 1525.   *Harmony by* M. PRAETORIUS, 1610.

The mouth of fools doth God con-fess, But while their lips draw nigh him

Their heart is full of wick-ed-ness, And all their deeds de-ny him.

Cor-rupt are they, and ev-'ry one A-bom-i-na-ble

deeds hath done; There is not one well-do—er.

1 Es spricht der Unweisen Mund wohl:
  Den rechten Gott wir meinen;
  Doch ist ihr Herz Unglaubens voll,
  Mit That sie ihn verneinen.
  Ihr Wesen ist verderbet zwar,
  Für Gott ist es ein Gräuel gar,
  Es thut ihr'r Keiner kein gut.

1 The mouth of fools doth God confess,
  But while their lips draw nigh him
  Their heart is full of wickedness,
  And all their deeds deny him.
  Corrupt are they, and every one
  Abominable deeds hath done ;
  There is not one well-doer.

2 Gott selbst vom Himmel sah herab
    Auf aller Menschen Kinder,
    Zu schauen sie er sich begab,
    Ob er Jemand wird finden,
    Der sein'n Verstand gerichtet hätt
    Mit Ernst, nach Gottes Worten thät
    Und fragt nach seinem Willen.

2 The Lord looked down from his high tower
    On all mankind below him,
    To see if any owned his power,
    And truly sought to know him;
    Who all their understanding bent
    To search his holy Word, intent
    To do his will in earnest.

3 Da war Niemand auf rechter Bahn,
    Sie war'n all' ausgeschritten;
    Ein Jeder ging nach seinem Wahn
    Und hielt verlor'ne Sitten.
    Es that ihm Keiner doch kein gut,
    Wie wohl gar viel betrog der Muth,
    Ihr Thun sollt' Gott gefallen.

3 But none there was who walked with God,
    For all aside had slidden,
    Delusive paths of folly trod,
    And followed lusts forbidden;
    Not one there was who practiced good,
    And yet they deemed, in haughty mood,
    Their deeds must surely please him.

4 Wie lang wollen unwissend sein
    Die solche Müh auflaben,
    Und fressen dafür das Volk mein
    Und nähr'n sich mit sei'm Schaden?
    Es steht ihr Trauen nicht auf Gott,
    Sie rufen ihm nicht in der Noth,
    Sie woll'n sich selbst versorgen.

4 How long, by folly blindly led,
    Will ye oppress the needy,
    And eat my people up like bread?
    So fierce are ye, and greedy!
    In God they put no trust at all,
    Nor will on him in trouble call,
    But be their own providers.

5 Darum ist ihr Herz nimmer still
    Und steht allzeit in Forchten;
    Gott bei den Frommen bleiben will,
    Dem sie mit Glauben g'horchen.
    Ihr aber schmäht des Armen Rath,
    Und höhnet alles, was er sagt,
    Daß Gott sein Trost ist worden.

5 Therefore their heart is never still,
    A falling leaf dismays them;
    God is with him who doth his will,
    Who trusts and obeys Him;
    But ye the poor man's hope despise,
    And laugh at him, e'en when he cries,
    That God is his sure comfort.

6 Wer soll Israel dem Armen
    Zu Zion Heil erlangen?
    Gott wird sich sein's Volk's erbarmen
    Und lösen, sie gefangen.
    Das wird er thun durch seinen Sohn,
    Davon wird Jakob Wonne ha'n
    Und Israel sich freuen.

6 Who shall to Israel's outcast race
    From Zion bring salvation?
    God will himself at length show grace,
    And loose the captive nation;
    That will he do by Christ their King;
    Let Jacob then be glad and sing,
    And Israel be joyful.

IV. Aus tiefer Noth schrei' ich zu dir.

Out of the Deep I Cry to Thee.

PSALM CXXX.—"*De profundis clamavi ad te.*"

FIRST MELODY, 1525.　　　　　　*Harmonized by* JOH. SEB. BACH.

Out of the deep I cry to thee; O Lord God, hear my cry - ing:
In - cline thy gra - cious ear to me, With pray'r to thee ap - ply - ing. For if thou

fix thy searching eye On all sin and in - i - qui - ty, Who, Lord, can stand be - fore thee?

SECOND MELODY, 1544.　　　　　　*Harmonized by* A. HAUPT, 1869.

Out of the deep I cry to thee; O Lord God, hear my cry - ing:
In - cline thy gra - cious ear to me, With pray'r to thee ap - ply - ing. For if thou fix thy

searching eye On all sin and in - i - qui - ty, Who, Lord, can stand be - fore thee?

Aus tiefer Noth schrei' ich zu dir.

Out of the Deep I Cry to Thee.

1 Aus tiefer Noth schrei' ich zu dir,
  Herr Gott, erhör' mein Rufen,
  Dein gnädig' Ohren kehr zu mir,
  Und meiner Bitt' sie öffnen.
  Denn so du willst das sehen an,
  Was Sünd' und Unrecht ist gethan,
  Wer kann, Herr, vor dir bleiben?

2 Bei dir gilt nichts denn Gnad' und Gunst
  Die Sünde zu vergeben.
  Es ist doch unser Thun umsonst,
  Auch in dem besten Leben.
  Vor dir Niemand sich rühmen kann,
  Des muß dich fürchten Jedermann
  Und deiner Gnade leben.

3 Darum auf Gott will hoffen ich,
  Auf mein Verdienst nicht bauen,
  Auf ihn mein Herz soll lassen sich,
  Und seiner Güte trauen,
  Die mir zusagt sein werthes Wort,
  Das ist mein Trost und treuer Hort,
  Des will ich allzeit harren.

4 Und ob es währt bis in die Nacht
  Und wieder an den Morgen,
  Doch soll mein Herz an Gottes Macht
  Verzweifeln nicht noch sorgen,
  So thu' Israel rechter Art,
  Der aus dem Geist erzeuget ward,
  Und seines Gott's erharre.

5 Ob bei uns ist der Sünden viel,
  Bei Gott ist viel mehr Gnaden;
  Sein' Hand zu helfen hat kein Ziel,
  Wie groß auch sei der Schaden.
  Er ist allein der gute Hirt,
  Der Israel erlö en wird
  Aus seinen Sünden allen.

1 Out of the deep I cry to thee ;
  O Lord God, hear my crying :
  Incline thy gracious ear to me,
  With prayer to thee applying.
  For if thou fix thy searching eye
  On all sin and iniquity,
  Who, Lord, can stand before thee ?

2 But love and grace with thee prevail,
  O God, our sins forgiving ;
  The holiest deeds can naught avail
  Of all before thee living.
  Before thee none can boast him clear ;
  Therefore must each thy judgment fear,
  And live on thy compassion.

3 For this, my hope in God shall rest,
  Naught building on my merit ;
  My heart confides, of him possest,
  His goodness stays my spirit.
  His precious word assureth me ;
  My solace, my sure rock is he,
  Whereon my soul abideth.

4 And though I wait the livelong night
  And till the morn returneth,
  My heart undoubting trusts his might
  Nor in impatience mourneth.
  Born of his Spirit, Israel
  In the right way thus fareth well,
  And on his God reposeth.

5 What though our sins are manifold ?
  Supreme his mercy reigneth ;
  No limit can his hand withhold,
  Where evil most obtaineth.
  He the good Shepherd is alone,
  Who Israel will redeem and own,
  Forgiving all transgression.

V. Ein neues Lied wir heben an.

By Help of God I fain would tell.

A Song of the Two Christian Martyrs burnt at Brussels by the Sophists of Louvain in the year MDXXII [July 1, 1523].

MELODY, 1525.   *Harmony by* M. PRAETORIUS, 1610.

{ By help of God I fain would tell   A new and won-drous sto - ry, }
{ And sing a mar - vel that be-fell   To his great praise and glo - ry. }

At Brus-sels in the Ne - ther-lands He hath His ban - ner lift - -

ed, To show his won - ders by the hands Of two youths,

high - ly gift - - ed With rich and heav'n - ly grac - es.

Ein neues Lied wir heben an.

By Help of God I fain would tell.

1 Ein neues Lied wir heben an,
Das walt' Gott unser Herre,
Zu singen was Gott hat gethan
Zu seinem Lob und Ehre.
Zu Brüssel in dem Niederland
Wohl durch zween junge Knaben
Hat er sein Wunder g'macht bekannt,
Die er mit seinen Gaben
So reichlich hat gezieret.

2 Der Erst' recht wohl Johannes heißt,
So reich an Gottes Hulden;
Sein Bruder Heinrich nach dem Geist,
Ein rechter Christ ohn' Schulden.
Von dieser Welt geschieden sind,
Sie ha'n die Kron' erworben,
Recht wie die frommen Gottes Kind
Für sein Wort sind gestorben,
Sein' Märt'rer sind sie worden.

3 Der alte Feind sie fangen ließ,
Erschreckt sie lang mit Dräuen,
Das Wort Gott man sie leuken hieß,
Mit List auch wollt' sie täuben,
Von Löwen der Sophisten viel,
Mit ihrer Kunst verloren,
Versammelt er zu diesem Spiel;
Der Geist sie macht zu Thoren,
Sie konnten nichts gewinnen.

4 Sie sungen süß, sie sungen sau'r,
Versuchten manche Listen;
Die Knaben standen wie ein' Mau'r,
Veracht'ten die Sophisten.
Den alten Feind das sehr verdroß,
Daß er war überwunden
Von solchen Jungen, er so groß;
Er ward voll Zorn von Stunden,
Gedacht' sie zu verbrennen.

1 By help of God I fain would tell
A new and wondrous story,
And sing a marvel that befell
To his great praise and glory.
At Brussels in the Netherlands
He hath his banner lifted,
To show his wonders by the hands
Of two youths, highly gifted
With rich and heavenly graces.

2 One of these youths was calléd John,
And Henry was the other ;
Rich in the grace of God was one,
A Christian true his brother.
For God's dear Word they shed their blood,
And from the world departed
Like bold and pious sons of God ;
Faithful and lion-hearted,
They won the crown of martyrs.

3 The old Arch-fiend did them immure,
To terrify them seeking ;
They bade them God's dear Word abjure,
And fain would stop their speaking.
From Louvain many Sophists came,
Deep versed in human learning,
God's Spirit foiled them at their game
Their pride to folly turning.
They could not but be losers.

4 They spake them fair, they spake them foul,
Their sharp devices trying.
Like rocks stood firm each brave young soul
The Sophists' art defying.
The enemy waxed fierce in hate,
And for their life-blood thirsted ;
He fumed and chafed that one so great
Should by two babes be worsted,
And straightway sought to burn them.

5 Sie raubten ihn'n das Klosterkleid,
   Die Weih' sie ihn'n auch nahmen;
   Die Knaben waren des bereit,
   Sie sprachen fröhlich: Amen!
   Sie dankten ihrem Vater, Gott,
   Daß sie los sollten werden
   Des Teufels Larvenspiel und Spott,
   Darin durch falsche Berden
   Die Welt er gar betreuget.

6 Da schickt Gott durch sein Gnad' also,
   Daß sie recht Priester worden:
   Sich selbst ihm mußten opfern da
   Und gehn im Christen Orden,
   Der Welt ganz abgestorben sein,
   Die Heuchelei ablegen,
   Zum Himmel kommen frei und rein,
   Die Möncherei ausfegen
   Und Menschen Tand hie lassen.

7 Man schrieb ihn'n für ein Brieflein klein,
   Das hieß man sie selbst lesen,
   Die Stück' sie zeigten alle drein,
   Was ihr Glaub' war gewesen.
   Der höchste Irrthum dieser war:
   Man muß allein Gott glauben,
   Der Mensch leugt und treugt immerdar,
   Dem soll man nichts vertrauen;
   Deß mußten sie verbrennen.

8 Zwei große Feur sie zünd'ten an,
   Die Knaben sie her brachten,
   Es nahm groß Wunder Jedermann,
   Daß sie solch' Pein verracht'ten,
   Mit Freuden sie sich gaben drein,
   Mit Gottes Lob und Singen,
   Der Muth ward den Sophisten klein
   Für diesen neuen Dingen,
   Da sich Gott ließ so merken.

9 Der Schimpf sie nun gereuet hat,
   Sie wollten's gern schön machen;
   Sie thürn nicht rühmen sich der That
   Sie bergen fast die Sachen,

---

5 Their monkish garb from them they take,
   And gown of ordination ;
   The youths a cheerful Amen spake,
   And showed no hesitation.
   They thanked their God that by his aid
   They now had been denuded
   Of Satan's mock and masquerade,
   Whereby he had deluded
   The world with false pretences.

6 Thus by the power of grace they were
   True priests of God's own making,
   Who offered up themselves e'en there,
   Christ's holy orders taking ;
   Dead to the world, they cast aside
   Hypocrisy's sour leaven,
   That penitent and justified
   They might go clean to heaven,
   And leave all monkish follies.

7 They then were told that they must read
   A note which was dictated ;
   They straightway wrote their fate and creed,
   And not one jot abated.
   Now mark their heresy ! "We must
   In God be firm believers ;
   In mortal men not put our trust,
   For they are all deceivers ;"
   For this they must be burned !

8 Two fires were lit ; the youths were brought,
   But all were seized with wonder
   To see them set the flames at naught,
   And stood as struck with thunder.
   With joy they came in sight of all,
   And sang aloud God's praises ;
   The Sophists' courage waxéd small
   Before such wondrous traces
   Of God's almighty finger.

9 The scandal they repent, and would
   Right gladly gloss it over ;
   They dare not boast their deed of blood,
   But seek the stain to cover.

Die Schand' im Herzen beißet sie
Und klagen's ihr'n Genossen,
Doch kann der Geist nicht schweigen hie:
Des Habels Blut vergossen,
Es muß den Kain melden.

They feel the shame within their breast,
And charge therewith each other;
But now the Spirit cannot rest,
For Abel 'gainst his brother
Doth cry aloud for vengeance.

10 Die Aschen will nicht lassen ab,
Sie stäubt in allen Landen;
Sie hilft kein Bach, Loch, Grub' noch Grab,
Sie macht den Feind zu Schanden.
Die er im Leben durch den Mord
Zu schweigen hat gedrungen,
Die muß er todt an allem Ort
Mit aller Stimm' und Zungen
Gar fröhlich lassen singen.

10 Their ashes will not rest; world-wide
They fly through every nation.
No cave nor grave, no turn nor tide,
Can hide th' abomination.
The voices which with cruel hands
They put to silence living,
Are heard, though dead, throughout all lands
Their testimony giving,
And loud hosannas singing.

11 Noch lassen sie ihr Lügen nicht,
Den großen Mord zu schmücken,
Sie gehen für ein falsch Gedicht,
Ihr Gewissen thut sie drücken,
Die Heil'gen Gott's auch nach dem Tod
Von ihn'n geläftert werden,
Sie sagen: in der letzten Noth
Die Knaben noch auf Erden
Sich sollen ha'n umkehret.

11 From lies to lies they still proceed,
And feign forthwith a story
To color o'er the murderous deed;
Their conscience pricks them sorely.
These saints of God e'en after death
They slandered, and asserted
The youths had with their latest breath
Confessed and been converted,
Their heresy renouncing.

12 Die laß man lügen immerhin,
Sie haben's keinen Frommen,
Wir sollen danken Gott darin,
Sein Wort ist wiederkommen.
Der Sommer ist hart für der Thür
Der Winter ist vergangen,
Die zarten Blümlein geh'n herfür:
Der das hat angefangen,
Der wird es wohl vollenden.

12 Then let them still go on and lie,
They cannot win a blessing;
And let us thank God heartily,
His Word again possessing.
Summer is even at our door,
The winter now has vanished,
The tender flowerets spring once more,
And he, who winter banished,
Will send a happy summer.

VI. Nun komm, der Heiden Heiland.

Saviour of the Heathen, known.

From the Ambrosian Christmas Hymn, "Veni, Redemptor, Gentium."

Melody derived from the Ambrosian original, 1525.

Harmony from "The Choral Book for England," by WM. STERNDALE BENNETT and OTTO GOLDSCHMIDT, 1865.

Sav - iour of the hea - then, known As the prom - ised vir - gin's Son;

Come, thou won - der of the earth, God or - dained thee such a birth.

1 Nun komm, der Heiden Heiland,
Der Jungfrauen Kind erkannt,
Daß sich wunder alle Welt,
Gott solch' Geburt ihm bestellt.

2 Nicht von Mann's Blut noch von Fleisch,
Allein von dem heil'gen Geist
Ist Gott's Wort worden ein Mensch,
Und blüht ein Frucht Weibes Fleisch.

3 Der Jungfrau Leib schwanger ward
Doch blieb Keuschheit rein bewahrt,
Leucht herfür manch Tugend schon,
Gott da war in seinem Thron.

1 Saviour of the heathen, known
As the promised virgin's Son ;
Come thou wonder of the earth,
God ordained thee such a birth.

2 Not of flesh and blood the son,
Offspring of the Holy One,
Born of Mary ever-blest,
God in flesh is manifest.

3 Cherished is the Holy Child
By the mother undefiled ;
In the virgin, full of grace,
God has made his dwelling-place.

4 Er ging aus der Kammer fein,
   Dem kön'glichen Saal so rein,
   Gott von Art und Mensch ein Held
   Sein'n Weg er zu laufen eilt.

5 Sein Lauf kam vom Vater her
   Und kehrt wieder zum Vater,
   Fuhr hinunter zu der Höll'
   Und wieder zu Gottes Stuhl.

6 Der du bist dem Vater gleich,
   Führ hinaus den Sieg im Fleisch,
   Daß dein ewig Gottes G'walt
   In uns das krank Fleisch enthalt.

7 Dein' Krippen glänzt hell und klar,
   Die Nacht giebt ein neu Licht dar,
   Dunkel muß nicht kommen d'rein
   Der Glaub' bleibt immer im Schein.

8 Lob sei Gott dem Vater g'than,
   Lob sei Gott dem ein'gen Sohn,
   Lob sei Gott dem heil'gen Geist,
   Immer und in Ewigkeit.

4 Lo! he comes! the Lord of all
   Leaves his bright and royal hall ;
   God and man, with giant force,
   Hastening to run his course.

5 To the Father whence he came
   He returns with brighter fame ;
   Down to hell he goes alone,
   Then ascends to God's high throne.

6 Thou, the Father's equal, win
   Victory in the flesh o'er sin ;
   So shall man, though weak and frail,
   By the indwelling God prevail.

7 On thy lowly manger night
   Sheds a pure unwonted light ;
   Darkness must not enter here,
   Faith abides in sunshine clear.

8 Praise be to the Father done,
   Praise be to the only Son,
   Praises to the Spirit be,
   Now and to eternity.

VII. Chriſtum wir ſollen loben ſchon.

Now praise we Christ, the Holy One.

From the Hymn " A solis ortûs cardine."

The Original Latin Melody. Harmony by M. PRAETORIUS, 1609.

Now praise we Christ, the Ho - ly One, The spot - less vir - gin Ma - ry's Son,

Far as the bless-ed sun doth shine, E'en to the world's re - mote con - fine.

1 Chriſtum wir ſollen loben ſchon
Der reinen Magd Marien Sohn,
So weit die liebe Sonne leucht't
Und an aller Welt Ende reicht.

2 Der ſelig Schöpfer aller Ding'
Zog an ein's Knechtes Leib gering,
Daß er das Fleiſch durch's Fleiſch erwürb',
Und ſein' Geſchöpf nicht all's verdürb'.

3 Die göttlich Gnad' vom Himmel groß
Sich in die keuſche Mutter goß;
Ein Mägdlein trug ein heimlich Pfand,
Das der Natur war unbekannt.

1 Now praise we Christ, the Holy One,
The spotless virgin Mary's Son,
Far as the blessèd sun doth shine,
E'en to the world's remote confine.

2 He, who himself all things did make,
A servant's form vouchsafed to take,
That He as man mankind might win,
And save His creatures from their sin.

3 The grace of God, th'Almighty Lord,
On the chaste mother was outpoured;
A virgin pure and undefiled
In wondrous wise conceived a child.

4 Das züchtig Haus des Herzens zart
Gar bald ein Tempel Gottes ward,
Die kein Mann rühret noch erkannt',
Von Gott's Wort man sie schwanger fand.

5 Die edle Mutter hat gebor'n,
Den Gabriel verhieß zuvorn,
Den Sanct Johann's mit Springen zeigt,
Da er noch lag im Mutter Leib.

6 Er lag im Heu mit Armuth groß,
Die Krippen hart ihn nicht verdroß,
Es ward ein kleine Milch sein Speis',
Der nie kein Böglein hungern ließ.

7 Des Himmels Chör' sich freuen drob,
Und die Engel singen Gott Lob,
Den armen Hirten wird vermelt't
Der Hirt und Schöpfer aller Welt.

8 Lob, Ehr und Dank sei dir gesagt,
Christe gebor'n von reinen Magd,
Mit Vater und dem heil'gen Geist
Von nun an bis in Ewigkeit!

4 The holy maid became th' abode
And temple of the living God;
And she, who knew not man, was blest
With God's own Word made manifest.

5 The noble mother bare a Son,
For so did Gabriel's promise run,
Whom John confest and leapt with joy,
Ere yet the mother knew her boy.

6 In a rude manger, stretched on hay,
In poverty content he lay;
With milk was fed the Lord of all,
Who feeds the ravens when they call.

7 Th' angelic choir rejoice, and raise
Their voice to God in songs of praise;
To humble shepherds is proclaimed
The Shepherd who the world hath framed.

8 Honor to thee, O Christ, be paid,
Pure offspring of a holy maid,
With Father and with Holy Ghost,
Till time in time's abyss be lost.

VIII. Gelobet sei'st du, Jesu Christ.

All Praise to Jesus' hallowed Name.

The first stanza an ancient German Christmas Hymn. Six stanzas added by Luther.

Ancient German Melody, in Walter, 1525.   *Harmony by A. HAUPT, 1869.*

All praise to Je - sus' hal - lowed name, Who of vir - gin

pure be - came True man for us! The an - gels sing As

the glad news to earth they bring.......... Hal - le - lu - jah!

1 Gelobet sei'st du, Jesu Christ,
Daß du Mensch geboren bist
Von einer Jungfrau, das ist wahr,
Deß freuet sich der Engel Schaar.
               Kyrioleis.

2 Des ew'gen Vaters einzig Kind
Jetzt man in der Krippen findt,
In unser armes Fleisch und Blut
Verkleidet sich das ewig Gut.
               Kyrioleis.

1 All praise to Jesus' hallowed name
Who of virgin pure became
True man for us! The angels sing
As the glad news to earth they bring.
               Hallelujah!

2 Th' eternal Father's only Son
For a manger leaves his throne.
Disguised in our poor flesh and blood
See now the everlasting Good.
               Hallelujah!

3 Den aller Welt Kreis nie beschloß,
Der liegt in Marien Schooß,
Er ist ein Kindlein worden klein,
Der alle Ding erhält allein.
            Kyrioleis.

4 Das ewig Licht geht da herein,
Gibt der Welt ein'n neuen Schein;
Es leucht't wohl mitten in der Nacht
Und uns des Lichtes Kinder macht.
            Kyrioleis.

5 Der Sohn des Vaters, Gott von Art,
Ein Gast in der Werlet ward,
Und führt uns aus dem Jammerthal;
Er macht uns Erben in sei'm Saal.
            Kyrioleis.

6 Er ist auf Erden kommen arm,
Daß er unser sich erbarm',
Und in dem Himmel machet reich
Und seinen lieben Engeln gleich.
            Kyrioleis.

7 Das hat er alles uns gethan,
Sein' groß' Lieb' zu zeigen an.
Deß freu' sich alle Christenheit
Und dank' ihm des in Ewigkeit.
            Kyrioleis.

3 He whom the world could not inwrap
Yonder lies in Mary's lap;
He is become an infant small,
Who by his might upholdeth all.
            Hallelujah!

4 Th' eternal Light, come down from heaven,
Hath to us new sunshine given;
It shineth in the midst of night,
And maketh us the sons of light.
            Hallelujah!

5 The Father's Son, God everblest,
In the world became a guest;
He leads us from this vale of tears,
And makes us in his kingdom heirs.
            Hallelujah!

6 He came to earth so mean and poor,
Man to pity and restore,
And make us rich in heaven above,
Equal with angels through his love.
            Hallelujah!

7 All this he did to show his grace
To our poor and sinful race;
For this let Christendom adore
And praise his name for evermore.
            Hallelujah!

IX. Christ lag in Todesbanden.

Christ was laid in Death's strong Bands.

"Christ ist erstanden."—[*Gebessert.*   D. MARTIN LUTHER.]

Melody derived from that of the older hymn, 1525.

Harmony by WM. STERNDALE BENNETT *and* OTTO GOLDSCHMITT, 1865.

Christ.. was laid in Death's strong bands For our trans - gres - sions giv - en.
Risen,.. at God's right hand he stands And brings us life from heav - en.

There - fore let us joy - ful be, Prais - ing God right thank - ful - ly

With loud songs of Hal - le - lu - jah! Hal - le - lu - jah!

1 Christ lag in Todesbanden
   Für unser' Sünd' gegeben;
   Der ist wieder erstanden
   Und hat uns bracht das Leben:
   Deß wir sollen fröhlich sein,
   Gott loben und dankbar sein,
   Und singen Halleluja!
              Halleluja!

2 Den Tod Niemand zwingen konnt'
   Bei allen Menschenkindern;
   Das macht alles unser' Sünd',
   Kein' Unschuld war zu finden.

1 Christ was laid in Death's strong bands
   For our transgressions givén.
   Risen, at God's right hand he stands
   And brings us life from heaven.
   Therefore let us joyful be
   Praising God right thankfully
   With loud songs of Hallelujah!
              Hallelujah!

2 None o'er Death could victory win;
   O'er all mankind he reignéd.
   'Twas by reason of our sin;
   There was not one unstainéd.

Davon kam der Tod so bald
Und nahm über uns Gewalt,
Hielt uns in sei'm Reich gefangen.
    Halleluja!

3 Jesus Christus, Gottes Sohn,
   An unser Statt ist kommen,
   Und hat die Sünde abgethan,
   Damit dem Tod genommen
   All sein Recht und sein' Gewalt,
   Da bleibt nichts denn Tod's Gestalt,
   Den Stachel hat er verloren.
    Halleluja!

4 Es war ein wunderlich Krieg,
   Da Tod und Leben rungen;
   Das Leben behielt den Sieg,
   Es hat den Tod verschlungen.
   Die Schrift hat verkündet das,
   Wie ein Tod den andern fraß,
   Ein Spott aus dem Tod ist worden.
    Halleluja!

5 Hie ist das recht' Osterlamm,
   Davon Gott hat geboten,
   Das ist an des Kreuzes Stamm
   In heißer Lieb' gebraten,
   Deß Blut zeichnet unser' Thür,
   Das hält der Glaub' dem Tod für,
   Der Würger kann uns nicht rühren.
    Halleluja!

6 So feiern wir das hoh' Fest
   Mit Herzens Freud' und Wonne,
   Das uns der Herr scheinen läßt,
   Er ist selber die Sonne,
   Der durch seiner Gnaden Glanz
   Erleucht't uns're Herzen ganz,
   Der Sünden Nacht ist vergangen.
    Halleluja!

7 Wir essen und leben wohl
   In rechten Osterfladen,
   Der alt' Sauerteig nicht soll
   Sein bei dem Wort der Gnaden,
   Christus will die Koste sein
   Und speisen die Seel' allein,
   Der Glaub' will kein's Andern Leben.
    Halleluja!

Thus came Death upon us all,
Bound the captive world in thrall,
Held us 'neath his dread dominion.
    Hallelujah!

3 Jesus Christ, God's only Son,
   To our low state descending,
   All our sins away hath done
   Death's power forever ending.
   Ruined all his right and claim
   Left him nothing but the name,
   For his sting is lost forever.
    Hallelujah!

4 Strange and dreadful was the fray,
   When Death and Life contended;
   But 'twas Life that won the day,
   And Death's dark sway was ended.
   Holy Scripture plainly saith,
   Death is swallowed up of Death,
   Put to scorn and led in triumph.
    Hallelujah!

5 This, the Paschal Lamb, the Christ,
   Whom God so freely gave us,
   On the cross is sacrificed
   In flames of love to save us.
   On our door the blood-mark ;—Faith
   Holds it in the face of Death.
   The Destroyer can not harm us.
    Hallelujah!

6 Therefore let us keep the feast
   With heartfelt exultation ;
   God to shine on us is pleased,
   The Sun of our salvation.
   On our hearts, with heavenly grace,
   Beams the brightness of his face,
   And the night of sin has vanished.
    Hallelujah!

7 Eat th' unleavened bread to-day,
   And drink the paschal chalice ;
   From God's pure word put away
   The leaven of guile and malice.
   Christ alone our souls will feed ;
   He is meat and drink indeed.
   Faith no other life desireth.
    Hallelujah!

X. Komm, Gott Schöpfer, Heiliger Geist.

Come, God Creator, Holy Ghost.

From the Hymn, "Veni, Creator Spiritus," ascribed to Charlemagne.

Melody, derived from the Latin original, 1543.

Harmony by JOHN SEBASTIAN BACH. *From the Cantata, „Gott der Hoffnung erfülle euch."*

Come, God Cre - a - tor, Ho - ly Ghost, And vis - it thou these souls of men;

Fill them with grac - es, as thou dost, Thy crea - tures make pure.... a - gain.

1 Komm, Gott Schöpfer, heiliger Geist,
   Besuch' das Herz der Menschen dein,
   Mit Gnaden sie füll', wie du weißt,
   Daß dein Geschöpf vorhin sein.

2 Denn du bist der Tröster genannt,
   Des Allerhöchsten Gabe theuer,
   Ein' geistlich' Salb' an uns gewandt,
   Ein lebend Brunn, Lieb' und Feuer.

3 Zünd' uns ein Licht an im Verstand,
   Gib uns in's Herz der Liebe Brunst,
   Das schwach' Fleisch' in uns, dir bekannt,
   Erhalt' fest' dein' Kräft' und Gunst.

4 Du bist mit Gaben siebenfalt
   Der Finger an Gott's rechter Hand;
   Des Vaters Wort giebst du gar bald
   Mit Zungen in alle Land.

5 Des Feindes List treibt von uns fern,
   Den Fried' schaff' bei uns deine Gnad',
   Daß wir dein'm Leiten folgen gern,
   Und meiden der Seelen Schad'.

6 Lehr' uns den Vater kennen wohl,
   Dazu Jesum Christ seinen Sohn,
   Daß wir des Glaubens werden voll,
   Dich beider Geist zu verstehen.

1 Come, God Creator, Holy Ghost,
   And visit thou these souls of men;
   Fill them with graces, as thou dost,
   Thy creatures make pure again.

2 For *Comforter* thy name we call.
   Sweet gift of God most high above,
   A holy unction to us all
   O Fount of life, Fire of love.

3 Our minds illumine and refresh,
   Deep in our hearts let love burn bright;
   Thou know'st the weakness of our flesh;
   And strengthen us with thy might.

4 Thou with thy wondrous sevenfold gifts
   The finger art of God's right hand;
   The Father's word thou sendest swift
   On tongues of fire to each land.

5 Drive far from us our wily foe;
   Grant us thy bless'd peace within,
   That in thy footsteps we may go,
   And shun the dark ways of sin.

6 Teach us the Father well to know,
   Likewise his only Son our Lord,
   Thyself to us believing show,
   Spirit of both, aye adored.

7 Gott Vater sei Lob und dem Sohn,
Der von den Todten auferstund;
Dem Tröster sei dasselb' gethan
In Ewigkeit alle Stund'.

7 Praise to the Father, and the Son
Who from the dead is risen again ;
Praise to the Comforter be done
Both now and ever. Amen.

XI. Jesus Christus unser Heiland, der den Tod.

Jesus Christ, who came to save.

A Song of Praise for Easter.

Melody in KLUG, 1535, *and* BAPST, 1543.
Originally Hypo-Dorian.

Harmony after JOHN SEBASTIAN BACH,
Condensed from a Choral-Vorspiel.

Je - sus Christ who came to save,....... And o - ver - came the grave, Is
now a - ris - en, And sin hath bound in pris - on. Ky - ri' e - lei - son.

1 Jesus Christus unser Heiland,
Der den Tod überwand,
Ist auferstanden,
Die Sünd' hat er gefangen.
Kyrie eleison !

2 Der ohn' Sünden war gebor'n,
Trug für uns Gottes Zorn,
Hat uns versöhnet,
Daß Gott uns sein' Huld gönnet.
Kyrie eleison !

3 Tod, Sünd', Leben und Genad,
All's in Händen er hat,
Er kann erretten
Alle, die zu ihm treten.
Kyrie eleison !

1 Jesus Christ, who came to save,
And overcame the grave,
Is now arisen,
And sin hath bound in prison.
Kyri' eleison !

2 Who withouten sin was found,
Bore our transgression's wound.
He is our Saviour,
And brings us to God's favor.
Kyri' eleison !

3 Life and mercy, sin and death,
All in his hands he hath ;
Them he'll deliver,
Who trust in him forever.
Kyri' eleison !

XII. Komm, heiliger Geist, Herre Gott.

Come, Holy Spirit, Lord our God.

"Veni, Sancte Spiritus, gebessert durch D. MARTIN LUTHER." *The last two stanzas added by Luther's hand.*

The original Latin Melody.

Harmony after ERYTHRAEUS, 1609.

Come, Ho - ly Spir - it, Lord.... our God, And pour thy gifts of....
O Lord, thou by thy heaven - ly light Dost gath - er and in....

grace...... a - broad; Thy faith - ful peo - ple..... fill.... with
faith...... u - nite Through all...... the world... a....... ho - ly

1st. blessing, Love's fire..... their hearts pos - sess - ing.
na - tion, To sing.... to thee with [OMIT......... ....] ex - ul

2nd.

ta - tion, Hal - le - lu - jah! Hal - le - lu - jah!

Komm, heiliger Geist, Herre Gott.

Come, Holy Spirit, Lord our God.

1 Komm, heiliger Geist, Herre Gott,
Erfüll' mit deiner Gnaden Gut
Deiner Gläubigen Herz, Muth und Sinn;
Dein brünst'ge Lieb' entzünd' in ihn'n.
O Herr, durch deines Lichtes Glast
Zu dem Glauben versammelt hast
Das Volk aus aller Welt Zungen,
Das sei dir, Herr, zu Lob gesungen,
    Halleluja! Halleluja!

2 Du heiliges Licht, edler Hort,
Laß uns leuchten des Lebens Wort,
Und lehr' uns Gott recht erkennen,
Von Herzen Vater ihn nennen.
O Herr, behüt' vor fremder Lehr,
Daß wir nicht Meister suchen mehr
Denn Jesum mit rechtem Glauben,
Und ihm aus ganzer Macht vertrauen.
    Halleluja! Halleluja!

3 Du heilige Brunst, süßer Trost,
Nun hilf uns fröhlich und getrost
In deinem Dienst beständig bleiben,
Die Trübsal uns nicht abtreiben.
O Herr, durch dein' Kraft uns bereit'
Und stärk des Fleisches Blödigkeit,
Daß wir hier ritterlich ringen,
Durch Tod und Leben zu dir dringen.
    Halleluja! Halleluja!

1 Come, Holy Spirit, Lord our God,
And pour thy gifts of grace abroad ;
Thy faithful people fill with blessing,
Love's fire their hearts possessing.
O Lord, thou by thy heavenly light
Dost gather and in faith unite
Through all the world a holy nation
To sing to thee with exultation,
    Hallelujah ! Hallelujah !

2 O holiest Light ! O Rock adored !
Give us thy light, thy living word,
To God himself our spirits leading,
With him as children pleading.
From error, Lord, our souls defend,
That they on Christ alone attend ,
In him with faith unfeigned abiding,
In him with all their might confiding.
    Hallelujah ! Hallelujah !

3 O holiest Fire ! O Source of rest !
Grant that with joy and hope possest,
And in thy service kept forever,
Naught us from thee may sever.
Lord, may thy power prepare each heart ;
To our weak nature strength impart,
Onward to press, our foes defying,
To thee, through living and through dying.
    Hallelujah ! Hallelujah !

NOTE.—The first stanza is found in a service-book of the church of Basel, of the year 1514. The irregularities of the German versification may be explained in part by the two-fold authorship, in this and other hymns.

XIII. Dieß sind die heil'gen zehn Gebot'.

That Men a godly Life might live.

Melody (from an old German Processional), Wittenberg, 1525.　　*Harmony by* M. PRAETORIUS, 1609.

1. That men a god-ly life might live, God did these ten com-mandments give By his true serv-ant Mo-ses, high Up-on the mount Si-na-i. Have mer-cy,............ Lord.

1 Dieß sind die heil'gen zehn Gebot',
Die uns gab unser Herre Gott
Durch Mosen, seinen Diener treu,
Hoch auf dem Berg Sinai.
　　　　Kyrioleis!

2 Ich bin allein dein Gott der Herr,
Kein' Götter sollst du haben mehr,
Du sollt mir ganz vertrauen dich,
Von Herzengrund lieben mich.
　　　　Kyrioleis!

3 Du sollt nicht brauchen zu Unehr'n
Den Namen Gottes, deines Herrn;
Du sollt nicht preisen recht noch gut,
Ohn' was Gott selbst red't und thut.
　　　　Kyrioleis!

4 Du sollt heil'gen den siebent' Tag,
Daß du und dein Haus ruhen mag,
Du sollt von dei'm Thun lassen ab,
Daß Gott sein Werk in dir hab'.
　　　　Kyrioleis!

1 That man a godly life might live,
God did these ten commandments give
By his true servant Moses, high
Upon the mount Sinai.
　　　　Have mercy, Lord.

2 I am thy God and Lord alone,
No other God besides me own ;
On my great mercy venture thee,
With all thy heart love thou me.
　　　　Have mercy, Lord.

3 By idle word and speech profane
Take not my holy name in vain ;
And praise not aught as good and true
But what God doth say and do.
　　　　Have mercy, Lord.

4 Hallow the day which God hath blest,
That thou and all thy house may rest ;
Keep hand and heart from labor free,
That God may so work in thee.
　　　　Have mercy, Lord.

5 Du sollt ehr'n und gehorsam sein
Dem Vater und der Mutter dein,
Und wo dein Hand ihn'n dienen kann,
So wirst du lang's Leben han.
Kyrioleis!

6 Du sollt nicht tödten zorniglich,
Nicht hassen noch selbst rächen dich,
Geduld haben und sanften Muth
Und auch dem Feind thun das Gut'.
Kyrioleis!

7 Dein' Eh' sollt du bewahren rein,
Daß auch dein Herz kein andere mein',
Und halten keusch das Leben dein
Mit Zucht und Mäßigkeit sein.
Kyrioleis!

8 Du sollt nicht stehlen Geld noch Gut,
Nicht wuchern Jemands Schweiß und Blut;
Du sollt aufthun dein' milde Hand
Den Armen in deinem Land.
Kyrioleis!

9 Du sollt kein falscher Zeuge sein,
Nicht lügen auf den Nächsten dein,
Sein' Unschuld sollt auch retten du
Und seine Schand' decken zu.
Kyrioleis!

10 Du sollt dein's Nächsten Weib und Haus
Begehren nicht, noch etwas d'raus,
Du sollt ihm wünschen alles Gut',
Wie dir dein Herz selber thut.
Kyrioleis!

11 Die Gebot, all' uns geben sind,
Daß du dein Sünd', o Menschenkind,
Erkennen sollt, und lernen wohl,
Wie man für Gott leben soll.
Kyrioleis!

12 Das helf' uns der Herr Jesus Christ,
Der unser Mittler worden ist:
Es ist mit unserm Thun verlor'n,
Verdienen doch eitel Zorn.
Kyrioleis!

5 Give to thy parents honor due,
Be dutiful and loving too;
And help them when their strength decays;
So shalt thou have length of days.
Have mercy, Lord.

6 Kill thou not out of evil will,
Nor hate, nor render ill for ill;
Be patient and of gentle mood,
And to thy foe do thou good.
Have mercy, Lord.

7 Be faithful to thy marriage vows,
Thy heart give only to thy spouse;
Keep thy life pure, and lest thou sin
Keep thyself with discipline.
Have mercy, Lord.

8 Steal not; oppressive acts abhor;
Nor wring their life-blood from the poor;
But open wide thy loving hand
To all the poor in the land.
Have mercy, Lord.

9 Bear not false witness, nor belie
Thy neighbor by foul calumny;
Defend his innocence from blame,
With charity hide his shame.
Have mercy, Lord.

10 Thy neighbor's wife desire thou not,
His house, nor aught that he hath got;
But wish that his such good may be
As thy heart doth wish for thee.
Have mercy, Lord.

11 God these commandments gave, therein
To show thee, son of man, thy sin,
And make thee also well perceive
How man for God ought to live.
Have mercy, Lord.

12 Help us, Lord Jesus Christ, for we
A Mediator have in thee;
Without thy help our works so vain
Merit naught but endless pain.
Have mercy, Lord.

XIV. Jeſus Chriſtus unſer Heiland, der von uns.

Christ, who freed our Souls from Danger.

"Improved" from the Communion Hymn of John Huss, " Jesus Christus, noster Salus."

Melody in Walter, 1525.

Harmony in VON TUCHER'S
" Schatz des Evangel. Kirchengesangs," 1848.

1. Christ, who freed our souls from dan - ger, And hath turn'd a - way God's an -

ger, Suffered pains no tongue can tell,...... To re - deem us from pains .. of hell.

1 Jeſus Chriſtus unſer Heiland,
Der von uns den Zorn Gottes wandt',
Durch das bitter' Leiden ſein
Half er uns aus der Hölle Pein.

2 Daß wir nimmer deß vergeſſen,
Gab er uns ſein' Leib zu eſſen,
Verborgen im Brot ſo klein,
Und zu trinken ſein Blut im Wein.

3 Wer ſich zu dem Tiſch will machen,
Der hab wohl acht auf ſein' Sachen:
Wer unwürdig hiezu geht,
Für das Leben den Tod empfäht.

1 Christ, who freed our souls from danger,
And hath turned away God's anger,
Suffered pains no tongue can tell,
To redeem us from pains of hell.

2 That we never might forget it,
Take my flesh, he said, and eat it,
Hidden in this piece of bread,
Drink my blood in this wine, he said.

3 Whoso to this board repaireth,
Take good heed how he prepareth ;
Death instead of life shall he
Find, who cometh unworthily.

4 Du sollt Gott den Vater preisen,
Daß er dich so wohl wollt' speisen,
Und für deine Missethat
In den Tod sein'n Sohn geben hat.

5 Du sollt glauben und nicht wanken,
Daß ein' Speise sei den Kranken,
Den'n ihr Herz' von Sünden schwer
Und für Angst ist betrübet sehr.

6 Solch' groß' Gnad' und Barmherzigkeit
Sucht ein Herz in großer Arbeit:
Ist dir wohl, so bleib' davon,
Daß du nicht kriegest bösen Lohn.

7 Er spricht selber: Kommt ihr Armen,
Laßt mich über euch erbarmen:
Kein Arzt ist dem Starken noth,
Sein' Kunst wird an ihm gar ein Spott.

8 Hätt'st du dir was konnt erwerben,
Was dürst' dann ich für dich sterben?
Dieser Tisch auch dir nicht gilt,
So du selber dir helfen willt.

9 Glaubst du das von Herzen Grunde
Und bekennest mit dem Munde,
So bist du recht wohl geschickt
Und die Speise dein' Seel' erquickt.

10 Die Frucht soll auch nicht ausbleiben:
Deinen Nächsten sollt du lieben,
Daß er dein genießen kann,
Wie dein Gott hat an dir gethan.

4 Praise the Father, God in heaven,
Who such dainty food hath given,
And for misdeeds thou hast done
Gave to die his belovéd Son.

5 Trust God's Word ; it is intended
For the sick who would be mended ;
Those whose heavy-laden breast
Groans with sin, and is seeking rest.

6 To such grace and mercy turneth
Every soul that truly mourneth ;
Art thou well ? Avoid this board,
Else thou reapest an ill reward.

7 Lo ! he saith himself, " Ye weary,
Come to me, and I will cheer ye ;"
Needless were the leech's skill
To the souls that be strong and well.

8 Couldst thou earn thine own salvation,
Useless were my death and passion ;
Wilt thou thine own helper be ?
No meet table is this for thee.

9 If thou this believest truly,
And confession makest duly,
Thou a welcome guest art here,
This rich banquet thy soul shall cheer.

10 Sweet henceforth shall be thy labor,
Thou shalt truly love thy neighbor
So shall he both taste and see
What thy Saviour hath done in thee.

XV. Gott sei gelobet und gebenedeiet.

May God be praised henceforth and blest forever.

Melody (from a more ancient German Hymn-tune),
Wittenberg, 1525.

Harmony by
H. SCHEIN, 1627.

May God be prais'd hence-forth and blest for - ev - er! Who, him - self both gift and
With his own flesh and blood our souls doth nour - ish; May they grow there - by and

giv - er, } Ky - ri' e - le - - i - son. By thy ho - ly bod - y, Lord,
flour - ish! }

the same Which from thine own moth - er.... Ma - ry.... came; By the drops

thou didst bleed, Help us in the hour of need! Ky - ri' e - le - - i - son.

Gott sei gelobet und gebenedeiet.

May God be praised henceforth and blest forever.

1 Gott sei gelobet und gebenedeiet,
Der uns selber hat gespeiset
Mit seinem Fleische und mit seinem Blute,
Das gib uns, Herr Gott, zu gute.
    Kyrieleison!
Herr, durch deinen heiligen Leichnam,
Der von deiner Mutter Maria kam,
Und das heilige Blut,
Hilf uns, Herr, aus aller Noth.
    Kyrieleison!

2 Der heilig' Leichnam ist für uns gegeben
Zum Tod, daß wir dadurch leben,
Nicht größer' Güte konnte er uns schenken,
Dabei wir sein soll'n gedenken.
    Kyrieleison!
Herr, dein Lieb' so groß dich zwungen hat,
Daß dein Blut an uns groß Wunder that
Und bezahlt unser Schuld,
Daß uns Gott ist worden hold.
    Kyrieleison!

3 Gott geb' uns Allen seiner Gnade Segen,
Daß wir gehen auf seinen Wegen,
In rechter Lieb' und brüderlicher Treue,
Daß uns die Speis' nicht gereue.
    Kyrieleison!
Herr, dein heilig' Geist uns nimmer laß,
Der uns geb' zu halten rechte Maß,
Daß dein' arm' Christenheit
Leb' in Fried' und Einigkeit.
    Kyrieleison!

1 May God be prais'd henceforth and blest
    forever!
Who, himself both gift and giver,
With his own flesh and blood our souls
    doth nourish;
May they grow thereby and flourish!
    Kyri' eleison!
By thy holy body, Lord, the same
Which from thine own mother Mary came,
By the drops thou didst bleed,
Help us in the hour of need!
    Kyri' eleison!

2 Thou hast to death thy holy body given,
Life to win for us in heaven;
By stronger love, dear Lord, thou couldst
    not bind us,
Whereof this should well remind us.
    Kyri' eleison!
Lord, thy love constrain'd thee for our good
Mighty things to do by thy dear blood;
Thou hast paid all we owed,
Thou hast made our peace with God.
    Kyri' eleison!

3 May God bestow on us his grace and
    blessing,
That, his holy footsteps tracing,
We walk as brethren dear in love and union,
Nor repent this sweet communion.
    Kyri' eleison!
Let not us the Holy Ghost forsake;
May he grant that we the right way take;
That thy poor church may see
Days of peace and unity.
    Kyri' eleison!

34

XVI. Es wollt' uns Gott genädig sein.

May God unto us gracious be.

PSALM LXVII. — "*Deus misereatur nostri.*"

Melody, Phrygian, 1538.　　　　　　　*Harmony by* A. HAUPT, 1869.

May God un-to us gra-cious be, And grant to us his bless-ing; Lord,

show thy face to us, through thee E-ter-nal life pos-sess-ing: That

all thy work and will, O God, To us may be re-veal-ed, And Christ's sal-va-tion

spread a-broad To hea-then lands un-seal-ed, And un-to God con-vert. them.

Es wollt' uns Gott genädig sein.

May God unto us gracious be.

1 Es wollt' uns Gott genädig sein,
　Und seinen Segen geben,
　Sein Antlitz uns mit hellem Schein
　Erleucht' zum ew'gen Leben,
　Daß wir erkennen seine Werk'
　Und was ihm b'liebt auf Erden,
　Und Jesus Christus Heil und Stärk'
　Bekannt den Heiden werden
　　Und sie zu Gott bekehren.

2 So danken, Gott, und loben dich
　Die Heiden überalle,
　Und alle Welt die freue sich
　Und sing' mit großem Schalle,
　Daß du auf Erden Richter bist
　Und läßt die Sünd' nicht walten,
　Dein Wort die Hut und Weide ist,
　Die alles Volk erhalten,
　　In rechter Bahn zu wallen.

3 Es danke, Gott, und lobe dich
　Das Volk in guten Thaten;
　Das Land bringt Frucht und bessert sich,
　Dein Wort ist wohl gerathen.
　Uns segen' Vater und der Sohn,
　Uns segen' Gott der heilig' Geist,
　Dem alle Welt die Ehre thu,
　Für ihm sich fürchte allermeist,
　　Nun sprecht von Herzen, Amen!

1 May God unto us gracious be,
　And grant to us his blessing;
　Lord, show thy face to us, through thee
　Eternal life possessing:
　That all thy work and will, o God,
　To us may be revealéd,
　And Christ's salvation spread abroad
　To heathen lands unsealéd,
　　And unto God convert them.

2 Thine over all shall be the praise
　And thanks of every nation,
　And all the world with joy shall raise
　The voice of exultation.
　For thou the sceptre, Lord, dost wield
　Sin to thyself subjecting;
　Thy Word, thy people's pasture-field,
　And fence their feet protecting,
　　Them in the way preserveth.

3 Thy fold, O God, shall bring to thee
　The praise of holy living;
　Thy word shall richly fruitful be,
　And earth shall yield thanksgiving.
　Bless us, O Father! bless, O Son!
　Grant, Holy Ghost, thy blessing!
　Thee earth shall honor—thee alone,
　Thy fear all souls possessing.
　　Now let our hearts say, *Amen*.

XVII. Wohl dem, der in Gottes Furcht steht.

Happy the Man who feareth God.

PSALM CXXVIII.—"*Beati omnes qui timent Dominum.*"

FIRST MELODY, 1525. *Harmony by* GESIUS, 1605.

Hap - py the man who fear - eth God, Whose feet his ho - ly ways have trod;

Thine own good hand shall nour-ish thee, And well and hap-py shalt........ thou be.

SECOND MELODY, 1537. *Harmony by* LANDGRAF MORITZ, 1612.

Also known by the title : Wo Gott zum Haus nicht gibt sein' Gunst.

Hap - py the man who fear - eth God, Whose feet his ho - ly ways have

trod ; Thine own good hand shall nour - ish thee, And well and hap - py shalt thou be.

Wohl dem, der in Gottes Furcht steht.

Happy the Man who feareth God.

1 Wohl dem, der in Gottesfurcht steht,
Und der auf seinem Wege geht;
Dein eigen Hand dich nähren soll,
So lebst du recht und geht dir wohl.

2 Dein Weib wird in dei'm Hause sein
Wie ein' Reben voll Trauben sein,
Und dein' Kinder um deinen Tisch
Wie Oelpflanzen, gesund und frisch.

2 Sich so reich Segen hängt dem an,
Wo in Gottes Furcht lebt ein Mann,
Von ihm läßt der alt' Fluch und Zorn,
Den Menschenkindern angebor'n.

4 Aus Zion wird Gott segnen dich,
Daß du wirst schauen stetiglich
Das Glück der Stadt Jerusalem,
Für Gott in Gnaden angenehm.

5 Fristen wird er das Leben dein
Und mit Güte stets bei dir sein,
Daß du sehen wirst Kindes Kind
Und daß Israel Friede findt.

1 Happy the man who feareth God,
Whose feet his holy ways have trod ;
Thine own good hand shall nourish thee,
And well and happy shalt thou be.

2 Thy wife shall, like a fruitful vine,
Fill all thy house with clusters fine ;
Thy children all be fresh and sound,
Like olive-plants thy table round.

3 Lo ! to the man these blessings cleave
Who in God's holy fear doth live ;
From him the ancient curse hath fled
By Adam's race inherited.

4 Out of Mount Zion God shall send,
And crown with joy thy latter end ;
That thou Jerusalem mayst see,
In favor and prosperity.

5 He shall be with thee in thy ways,
And give thee health and length of days ;
Yea, thou shalt children's children see,
And peace on Israel shall be.

XVIII. Mitten wir im Leben sind.

Though in Midst of Life we be.

Melody, 1525.   *Harmony by* ERYTHRAEUS, 1608.

{ Though in midst of life we be,.. Snares of death sur - round us;
{ Where shall we for suc - cor flee,.. Lest our foes con- [OMIT....... found us? To

thee, a - lone, our Sav - iour. We mourn our griev-ous sin which hath.... Stirred the fire of

thy fierce wrath. Ho - ly and gra-cious God! Ho - ly and mighty God! Ho - ly and

all - mer - ci - ful Sav - - iour! Thou e - ter - nal God. Save us, Lord, from

sink - ing In the deep and bit - ter flood. Ky - ri - e e - lei - - son.

Mitten wir im Leben sind.

Though in Midst of Life we be.

1 Mitten wir im Leben sind
  Mit dem Tod umfangen,
  Wen such'n wir der Hülfe thu',
  Daß wir Gnad' erlangen?
  Das bist du, Herr, alleine.
  Uns reuet unser' Missethat,
  Die dich, Herr, erzürnet hat.
    Heiliger Herre Gott,
    Heiliger, starker Gott,
    Heiliger, barmherziger Heiland,
    Du ewiger Gott!
  Laß uns nicht versinken
  In der bittern Todesnoth.
      Kyrieleison!

2 Mitten in den Tod ansieht
  Uns der Höllen Rachen;
  Wer will uns aus solcher Noth
  Frei und ledig machen?
  Das thust du, Herr, alleine.
  Es jammert dein' Barmherzigkeit
  Unser' Sünd' und großes Leid.
    Heiliger Herre Gott!
    Heiliger, starker Gott!
    Heiliger, barmherziger Heiland!
    Du ewiger Gott!
  Laß uns nicht verzagen
  Für der tiefen Höllenglut.
      Kyrieleison!

3 Mitten in der Höllen Angst
  Unser' Klag' uns treiben;
  Wo soll'n wir denn fliehen hin,
  Da wir mögen bleiben?
  Zu dir, Herr Christ, alleine.
  Vergossen ist dein theures Blut,
  Das g'nug für die Sünde thut.
    Heiliger Herre Gott!
    Heiliger, starker Gott!
    Heiliger, barmherziger Heiland!
    Du ewiger Gott!
  Laß uns nicht entfallen
  Von des rechten Glaubens Trost.
      Kyrieleison!

1 Though in midst of life we be,
  Snares of death surround us;
  Where shall we for succor flee,
  Lest our foes confound us?
  To thee alone, our Saviour.
  We mourn our grievous sin which hath
  Stirr'd the fire of thy fierce wrath.
    Holy and gracious God!
    Holy and mighty God!
    Holy and all-merciful Saviour!
    Thou eternal God!
  Save us, Lord, from sinking
  In the deep and bitter flood.
      Kyrie eleison.

2 Whilst in midst of death we be,
  Hell's grim jaws o'ertake us;
  Who from such distress will free.
  Who secure will make us?
  Thou only, Lord, canst do it!
  It moves thy tender heart to see
  Our great sin and misery.
    Holy and gracious God!
    Holy and mighty God!
    Holy and all merciful Saviour!
    Thou eternal God!
  Let not hell dismay us
  With its deep and burning flood.
      Kyrie eleison.

3 Into hell's fierce agony
  Sin doth headlong drive us:
  Where shall we for succor flee,
  Who, O, who will hide us?
  Thou only, blessèd Saviour.
  Thy precious blood was shed to win
  Peace and pardon for our sin.
    Holy and gracious God!
    Holy and mighty God!
    Holy and all-merciful Saviour!
  Let us not, we pray,
  From the true faith's comfort
  Fall in our last need away.
      Kyrie eleison.

XIX. Nun bitten wir den heiligen Geist.

Now pray we all God, the Comforter.

The first stanza from an ancient German hymn. The other stanzas added by Luther.

elody of the thirteenth Century.　　　　　　　　*Harmony by A. HAUPT, 1869.*

Now pray we all God, the Com - fort - er, In - to ev - ery

heart true faith to pour, And that he de - fend.... us, Yea, till death tend us,

When for heav'n we leave this world of sor - row. Have mer - cy, Lord.

1　Nun bitten wir den heiligen Geist
　Um den rechten Glauben allermeist,
　Daß er uns behüte an unserm Ende,
　Wann wir heimfahr'n aus diesem Elende.
　　　　　　Kyrioleis!

2　Du werthes Licht, gib uns deinen Schein,
　Lehr' uns Jesum Christ kennen allein,
　Daß wir an ihm bleiben, dem treuen Heiland,
　Der uns bracht hat zum rechten Vaterland.
　　　　　　Kyrioleis!

3　Du süße Lieb', schenk uns deine Gunst,
　Laß uns empfinden der Liebe Brunst,
　Daß wir uns von Herzen einander lieben
　Und in Frieden auf einem Sinn bleiben.
　　　　　　Kyrioleis!

1　Now pray we all God, the Comforter,
　Into every heart true faith to pour
　And that he defend us, Till death here end us,
　When for heaven we leave this world of sorrow.
　　　　　　Have mercy, Lord.

2　Shine into us, O most holy Light,
　That we Jesus Christ may know aright;
　Stayed on him forever, Our only Saviour,
　Who to our true home again hath brought us.
　　　　　　Have mercy, Lord.

3　Spirit of love, now our spirits bless;
　Them with thy own heavenly fire possess;
　That in heart uniting, In peace delighting,
　We may henceforth all be one in spirit.
　　　　　　Have mercy, Lord.

4 Du höchster Tröster in aller Noth,
   Hilf, daß wir nicht fürchten Schand noch Tod,
   Daß in uns die Sinne nicht verzagen,
   Wenn der Feind wird das Leben verklagen.
          Kyrioleis!

4 Our highest comfort in all distress !
   O let naught with fear our hearts oppress :
   Give us strength unfailing O'er fear prevail-
      ing,
   When th' accusing foe would overwhelm us.
          Have mercy, Lord.

XX. Mit Fried' und Freud' ich fahr' dahin.

In Peace and Joy I now depart.

A Song of Simeon, " Nunc Dimittis."

Melody, 1525.   *Harmony by* M. PRAETORIUS, 1610.

In peace and joy I now de-part, At God's dis - pos -
ing; For full of com - fort is.... my heart, Soft re - p os - ing.
So the Lord.... hath prom-is'd me, And death is but a slum - ber.

1 Mit Fried' und Freud' ich fahr' dahin,
     In Gottes Wille,
   Getrost ist mir mein Herz und Sinn,
     Sanft und stille.
   Wie Gott mir verheißen hat:
   Der Tod ist mein Schlaf worden.

1 In peace and joy I now depart,
     At God's disposing;
   For full of comfort is my heart,
     Soft reposing.
   So the Lord hath promis'd me,
   And death is but a slumber.

In peace and joy I now de-part, At God's dis-pos-ing; For full of com-fort is.... my heart, Soft re-pos-ing. So the Lord.... hath prom-is'd me, And death is but a slum-ber.

2 Das macht Christus, wahr Gottes Sohn,
   Der treue Heiland,
   Den du mich, Herr, hast sehen lan
   Und macht bekannt,
   Daß er sei das Leben
   Und Heil in Noth und Sterben.

3 Den hast du Allen fürgestellt
   Mit großen Gnaden;
   Zu seinem Reich die ganze Welt
   Heißen laden
   Durch dein theuer heilsam Wort,
   An allem Ort erschollen.

4 Er ist das Heil und selig Licht
   Für alle Heiden,
   Zu 'rleuchten, die dich kennen nicht
   Und zu weiden,
   Er ist dein's Volks Israel
   Der Preis, Ehr', Freud' und Wonne.

2 'Tis Christ that wrought this work for me,
   The faithful Saviour;
   Whom thou hast made mine eyes to see
   By thy favor.
   In him I behold my life,
   My help in need and dying.

3 Him thou hast unto all set forth,
   Their great salvation,
   And to his kingdom called the earth—
   Every nation.
   By thy dear, health-giving word,
   In every land resounding.

4 He is the Health and blessèd Light
   Of lands benighted,
   By him are they who dwelt in night
   Fed and lighted.
   While his Israel's hope he is,
   Their joy, reward and glory.

XXI. Menſch, willt du leben ſeliglich.

Wilt thou, O Man, live happily.

The Ten Commandments, abridged.

Melody, 1525.   *Harmony by* H. SCHEIN, 1627.

Wilt thou, O man, live hap - pi - ly, And dwell with God e - ter - - nal - ly,

The ten commandments keep, for thus Our God him - self bid - deth us. Kyr' e - lei - son.

1 Menſch, willt du leben ſeliglich,
Und bei Gott bleiben ewiglich,
Sollt du halten die zehn Gebot,
Die uns geben unſer Gott.
    Kyrioleis!

2 Dein Gott allein und Herr bin ich,
Kein ander Gott ſoll irren dich;
Trauen ſoll mir das Herze dein,
Mein eigen Reich ſollt du ſein.
    Kyrioleis!

3 Du ſollt mein'n Namen ehren ſchon
Und in der Noth mich rufen an,
Du ſollt heil'gen den Sabbath-Tag,
Das ich in dir wirken mag.
    Kyrioleis!

4 Dem Vater und der Mutter dein
Sollt du nach mir gehorſam ſein;
Niemand tödten noch zornig ſein,
Und deine Eh' halten rein.
    Kyrioleis!

5 Du ſollt ein'm andern ſtehlen nicht,
Auf Niemand falſches zeugen icht;
Deines Nächſten Weib nicht begehr'n
Und all ſein's Gut's gern entbehr'n.
    Kyrioleis!

1 Wilt thou, O man, live happily,
And dwell with God eternally,
The ten commandments keep, for thus
Our God himself biddeth us.
    Kyr' eleison!

2 I am the Lord and God! take heed
No other god doth thee mislead ;
Thy heart shall trust alone in me,
My kingdom then thou shalt be.
    Kyr' eleison!

2 Honor my name in word and deed,
And call on me in time of need:
Hallow the Sabbath, that I may
Work in thy heart on that day.
    Kyr' eleison!

4 Obedient always, next to me,
To father and to mother be ;
Kill no man : even anger dread ;
Keep sacred thy marriage-bed.
    Kyr' eleison!

5 Steal not, nor do thy neigbor wrong
By bearing witness with false tongue ;
Thy neighbor's wife desire thou not,
Nor grudge him aught he hath got.
    Kyr' eleison!

XXII. Gott der Vater wohn' uns bei.

God the Father, with us stay.

Adapted from an ancient German Litany.

Ancient German Melody.   *Harmony by* LANDGRAF MORITZ, 1612.

{ God the Father, with us stay, Nor suf-fer us to per-ish;}
{ All our sins, O take a-way, Us dy-ing, cheer and cher-ish. } From the pow'r of hell de-fend;

This grace to us be grant-ed:—Up-on thee to be plant-ed, In heart-felt faith un-daunted,

Trusting thee unto the end; With saints of ev-'ry na- - tion, Es-cap-ing hell's temp-ta- - tion,

Kept by the Lord's sal-va- - tion. A-men! A-men! Answer send! So sing we all Hal-le-lu-jah!

Gott der Vater wohn' uns bei.

God the Father, with us stay.

1 Gott der Vater wohn' uns bei
Und laß uns nicht verderben,
Mach' uns aller Sünden frei
Und helf' uns selig sterben.
Für dem Teufel uns bewahr,
Halt' uns bei festem Glauben,
Und auf dich laß uns bauen,
Aus Herzen Grund vertrauen,
Dir uns laffen ganz und gar;
Mit allen rechten Chriften
Entfliehen Teufels Liften,
Mit Waffen Gott's uns friften.
Amen! Amen! das sei wahr,
So fingen wir, Halleluja!

2 Jefus Chriftus wohn' uns bei
Und laß uns nicht verderben,
Mach' uns aller Sünden frei
Und helf' uns selig sterben.
Für dem Teufel uns bewahr,
Halt' uns bei festem Glauben,
Und auf dich laß uns bauen,
Aus Herzen Grund vertrauen,
Dir uns laffen ganz und gar;
Mit allen rechten Chriften
Entflieh'n des Teufels Liften,
Mit Waffen Gott's uns friften.
Amen! Amen! das sei wahr,
So fingen wir, Halleluja!

3 Der heilig' Geift wohn uns bei,
Und laß uns nicht verderben,
Mach' uns aller Sünden frei
Und helf' uns selig sterben.
Für dem Teufel uns bewahr,
Halt' uns bei festem Glauben,
Und auf dich laß uns bauen,
Aus Herzen Grund vertrauen,
Dir uns laffen ganz und gar;
Mit allen rechten Chriften
Entfliehen Teufels Liften,
Mit Waffen Gott's uns friften.
Amen! Amen! das sei wahr,
So fingen wir, Halleluja!

1 God, the Father, with us stay,
Nor suffer us to perish ;
All our sins O take away,
Us dying, cheer and cherish.
From the power of hell defend ;
This grace to us be granted :—
Upon thee to be planted,
In heartfelt faith undaunted,
Trusting thee unto the end ;
With saints of every nation,
Escaping hell's temptation,
Kept by the Lord's salvation.
Amen! Amen! Answer send !
So sing we all Hallelujah !

2 Jesus, Saviour with us stay,
Nor suffer us to perish ;
All our sins O take away,
Us dying, cheer and cherish.
From the power of hell defend ;
This grace to us be granted :—
Upon thee to be planted,
In heartfelt faith undaunted,
Trusting thee unto the end ;
With saints of every nation,
Escaping hell's temptation,
Kept by the Lord's salvation.
Amen! Amen! Answer send !
So sing we all Hallelujah !

3 Holy Spirit, with us stay,
Nor suffer us to perish ;
All our sins O take away,
Us dying, cheer and cherish.
From the power of hell defend ;
This grace to us be granted : --
Upon thee to be planted,
In heartfelt faith undaunted,
Trusting thee unto the end ;
With saints of every nation,
Escaping hell's temptation,
Kept by the Lord's salvation.
Amen! Amen! Answer send !
So sing we all Hallelujah !

XXIII. Wir glauben All' an einen Gott.

We all believe in one true God.

This hymn and tune were intended by Luther to be sung as the Creed during the morning service ("the German Mass"), and remained in such use for a long time.

Melody, 1525.

Harmony from BENNETT *and* GOLDSCHMIDT'S
"Choral Book for England," and there ascribed to an ancient source.

We all...... be-lieve in one true.... God, Ma-ker of the earth and heav-en,

The Fa-ther who to us the power To be-come his sons hath giv - en.

He will us at all times nour - ish, Soul and bod - y, guard us, guide us,

'Mid all harms will keep and cher - ish, That no ill shall e'er be - tide us.

He watch-es o'er us day and night,........ ...... All things are governed by his might.

1 Wir glauben All' an einen Gott,
  Schöpfer Himmels und der Erden,
  Der sich zum Vater geben hat,
  Daß wir seine Kinder werden.
  Er will uns allzeit ernähren,
  Leib und Seel' auch wohl bewahren,
  Allem Unfall will er wehren,
  Kein Leid soll uns widerfahren,
  Er sorget für uns, hüt't und wacht,
  Es steht Alles in seiner Macht.

2 Wir glauben auch an Jesum Christ,
  Seinen Sohn und unser'n Herren,
  Der ewig bei dem Vater ist,
  Gleicher Gott von Macht und Ehren,
  Von Maria der Jungfrauen
  Ist ein wahrer Mensch geboren
  Durch den heil'gen Geist im Glauben,
  Für uns, die wir war'n verloren,
  Am Kreuz gestorben, und vom Tod
  Wieder auferstanden durch Gott.

3 Wir glauben an den heil'gen Geist,
  Gott mit Vater und dem Sohne,
  Der aller Blöden Tröster heißt
  Und mit Gaben zieret schöne
  Die ganz' Christenheit auf Erden,
  Hält in einem Sinn gar eben,
  Hie all' Sünd' vergeben werden,
  Das Fleisch soll auch wieder leben.
  Nach diesem Elend ist bereit
  Uns ein Leben in Ewigkeit.

1 We all believe in one true God,
  Maker of the earth and heaven,
  The Father who to us the power
  To become his sons hath given.
  He will us at all times nourish,
  Soul and body, guard us, guide us,
  'Mid all harms will keep and cherish,
  That no ill shall ever betide us.
  He watches o'er us day and night;
  All things are governed by his might.

2 And we believe in Jesus Christ,
  Lord and Son of God confesséd,
  From everlasting days with God,
  In like power and glory blesséd.
  By the Holy Ghost conceivéd,
  Born of Mary, virgin mother,
  That to lost men who believéd
  He should Saviour be and brother;
  Was crucified, and from the grave,
  Through God, is risén, strong to save.

3 We in the Holy Ghost believe,
  Who with Son and Father reigneth,
  One true God. He, the Comforter,
  Feeble souls with gifts sustaineth.
  All his saints, in every nation,
  With one heart this faith receiving,
  From all sin obtain salvation,
  From the dust of death reviving.
  These sorrows past, there waits in store
  For us, the life for evermore.

48

XXIV. Wär' Gott nicht mit uns.

Had God not come, may Israel say.

PSALM CXXIV.—"*Nisi quia Dominus.*"

Melody, 1525.   *Harmony by* M. PRAETORIUS, 1610.

Had God not come, may Is - rael say, Had God not come to

aid.... us, Our en - e - mies on that sad day -Would sure - ly have dis -

mayed .. us; A rem - nant now, and hand - ful small, Held

in con - tempt and scorn by all, Who cru - el - ly op - press... us.

Wär' Gott nicht mit uns.

Had God not come, may Israel say.

1 Wär' Gott nicht mit uns diese Zeit,
  So soll Israel sagen,
  Wär' Gott nicht mit uns diese Zeit,
  Wir hätten mußt verzagen:
  Die so ein armes Häuflein sind,
  Veracht't von so viel Menschen=Kind,
  Die an uns setzen alle.

2 Auf uns ist so zornig ihr Sinn,
  Wo Gott hätt' das zugeben,
  Verschlungen hätten sie uns hin
  Mit ganzem Leib und Leben.
  Wir wär'n als die ein' Fluth ersäuft
  Und über die groß' Wasser läuft
  Und mit Gewalt verschwemmet.

3 Gott Lob und Dank, der nicht zugab,
  Daß ihr Schlund uns möcht' fangen,
  Wie ein Vogel des Stricks kommt ab,
  Ist unser' Seel' entgangen.
  Strick ist entzwei, und wir sind frei,
  Des Herren Namen steht uns bei,
  Des Gott's Himmels und Erden.

1 Had God not come, may Israel say,
  Had God not come to aid us,
  Our enemies on that sad day
  Would surely have dismayed us;
  A remnant now, and handful small,
  Held in contempt and scorn by all
  Who cruelly oppress us.

2 Their furious wrath, did God permit,
  Would surely have consumed us,
  And in the deep and yawning pit
  With life and limb entombed us;
  Like men o'er whom dark waters roll,
  The streams had gone e'en o'er our soul,
  And mightily o'erwhelmed us.

3 Thanks be to God, who from the pit
  Snatched us, when it was gaping;
  Our souls, like birds that break the net,
  To the blue skies escaping;
  The snare is broken—we are free!
  The Lord our helper praiséd be,
  The God of earth and heaven.

XXV. Zesaia, dem Propheten, das geschah.

These Things the Seer Isaiah did befall.

The German Sanctus.   *Written for Luther's German Mass, 1526.*

Melody, 1526.   *Harmony by* ERYTHRAEUS, 1608.

These things the seer I - sai - ah did be - fall: In spir - it he be - held the
Je = sai = a, dem Pro = phe = ten, das ge = schah, Daß er im Geist den Her = ren

Lord of all On a high throne, raised up in splen-dor bright, His gar - ment's
fi = tzen sah Auf ei = nem ho = hen Thron, in hel = lem Glanz, Sei = nes Klei=

bord - er filled the choir with light. Be - side him stood two ser - a - phim which had
des Saum den Chor fül = let ganz. Es stun=den zween Se=raph bei ihm dar = an,

Six wings, wherewith they both a - like were clad; With twain they hid their shin-ing
Sechs Flü = gel sah er ei = nen je = den han; Mit zween ver = bar = gen sie ihr

face, with twain They hid their feet as with a flow - ing train, And with the
Ant = lię klar, Mit zween be = ded = ten fie bie Fü = ße gar, Und mit den

oth - er twain they both did fly. One to the oth - er thus a - loud did cry:
an = dern zween fie flo = gen frei; Cen an = der ruf = ten fie mit gro = ßem G'fchrei:

Three times.

"Ho - ly is God, the Lord of Sa - ba - oth! His glo - ry
„Hei = lig ift Gott, der Her = re Ze = ba = oth! Sein' Chr' die

fill - eth all the trem - bling earth!" With the loud cry the posts and
gan = ze Welt er = fül = let hat!" Von dem G'fchrei zit = tert Schwell' und

thresh - olds shook, And the whole house was filled with mist and smoke.
Bal = ken gar, Das Haus auch ganz voll Rauch und Ne = bel war.

XXVI. Ein' feſte Burg iſt unſer Gott.

Strong Tower and Refuge is our God.

Psalm XLVI. — "*Deus noster refugium et virtus.*"

Melody, 1529.

Strong tower and ref - uge is our God, Right good - ly shield and wea - pon;

He helps us free in ev - ery need, That hath us now o'er - tak - en.

The old... e - vil foe Means us dead - ly woe; Deep guile and great... might

Are his dread arms in fight; On earth is not his e - qual.

Note.—The perfectly regular though rugged versification of the original text (8,7 ; 8,7; 5,5,5,6,7.) has been modified in later editions by an attempt to extend the shorter lines by one syllable. The genuine text is here given, and the English version is conformed to it.

Ein' feſte Burg iſt unſer Gott.

Strong Tower and Refuge is our God.

1 Ein' feſte Burg iſt unſer Gott,
　　Ein' gute Wehr und Waffen,
　　Er hilft uns frei aus aller Noth,
　　Die uns jetzt hat betroffen.
　　　Der alt' böſe Feind,
　　　Mit Ernſt er's jetzt meint:
　　　Groß Macht und viel Liſt,
　　　Sein' grauſam Rüſtung iſt,
　　　Auf Erd' iſt nicht ſein gleichen.

2 Mit unſer' Macht iſt nichts gethan,
　　Wir ſind gar bald verloren,
　　Es ſtreit't für uns der rechte Mann,
　　Den Gott hat ſelbſt erforen.
　　　Fragſt du, wer der iſt?
　　　Er heißt Jeſu Chriſt,
　　　Der Herr Zebaoth,
　　　Und iſt kein ander' Gott,
　　　Das Feld muß er behalten.

3 Und wenn die Welt voll Teufel wär,
　　Und wollt' uns gar verſchlingen,
　　So fürchten wir uns nicht ſo ſehr,
　　Es ſoll uns doch gelingen.
　　　Der Fürſt dieſer Welt,
　　　Wie ſaur er ſich ſtellt
　　　Thut er uns doch nicht,
　　　Das macht, er iſt gericht't;
　　　Ein Wörtlein kann ihn fällen.

4 Das Wort ſie ſollen laſſen ſtahn,
　　Und kein'n Dank dazu haben;
　　Er iſt bei uns wohl auf dem Plan
　　Mit ſeinem Geiſt und Gaben.
　　　Nehmen ſie den Leib,
　　　Gut, Ehr', Kind und Weib,
　　　Laß fahren dahin,
　　　Sie haben's kein'n Gewinn,
　　　Das Reich muß uns doch bleiben.

1 Strong tower and refuge is our God,
　　Right goodly shield and weapon;
　　He helps us free in every need,
　　That hath us now o'ertaken.
　　　The old evil foe,
　　　Means us deadly woe;
　　　Deep guile and great might
　　　Are his dread arms in fight;
　　　On earth is not his equal.

2 With our own might we nothing can,
　　Soon are we lost and fallen;
　　But for us fights the righteous man,
　　Whom God himself hath callen.
　　　Ask ye, Who is this?
　　　Jesus Christ it is,
　　　Our sole King and Lord,
　　　As God of Hosts adored;
　　　He holds the field forever.

3 Though earth all full of devils were,
　　Wide roaring to devour us;
　　Yet fear we no such grievous fear,
　　They shall not overpower us.
　　　This world's prince may still
　　　Scowl fierce as he will,
　　　He can harm us none,
　　　He's judged; the deed is done;
　　　One little word can fell him.

4 His Word they still shall let abide,
　　And little thank have for it;
　　Through all the fight he's on our side
　　With his good gifts and Spirit.
　　　Take they then our life,
　　　Wealth, fame, child and wife,
　　　Let these all be gone,
　　　No triumph have they won.
　　　The kingdom ours remaineth.

XXVII. Verleih' uns Frieden gnädiglich.

In these our Days so perilous.

" Da pacem Domine."

Melody, 1543.   Harmony by ERYTHRAEUS, 1608.

In these our days so per - - il - - ous, Lord, peace in mer - cy

send .. us; No God but thee can fight for us, No God but thee...... de -

fend.. us; Thou, our .... on - ly God and Sav - - iour.

Verleih' uns Frieden gnädiglich,	In these our days so perilous,
Herr Gott, zu unser'n Zeiten,	Lord, peace in mercy send us ;
Es ist doch ja kein Ander' nicht,	No God but thee can fight for us,
Der für uns könnte streiten,	No God but thee defend us ;
Denn du, unser Gott alleine.	Thou our only God and Saviour.

XXVIII. Herr Gott, dich loben wir.

Lord God, thy Praise we sing.

Te Deum Laudamus. For two Choirs.

Melody, from the Latin Melody. *Harmony by* LANDGRAF MORITZ.

FIRST CHOIR.   **SECOND CHOIR.**

Lord God, thy praise we sing; Lord God, our thanks we bring;
Herr Gott, dich lo = ben wir, Herr Gott, wir dan = ken dir!

Fa - ther in e - ter - ni - ty, All the world wor - ships thee.
Dich, Va = ter in E = wig = feit, Ehrt die Welt weit und breit.

An - gels all and heaven - ly host Of thy glo - ry loud - ly boast;
All' En = gel und Him = mels Heer' Und was die = net dei = ner Ehr',

Both Che - ru - bim and Ser - a - phim Sing ev - er with loud voice this hymn:
Auch Che = ru = bin und Se = ra = phin Sin = gen im = mer mit ho = her Stimm':

FIRST CHOIR. **SECOND CHOIR.**

Ho - ly art thou, our God! Ho - ly art thou, our God!
Hei = lig ift un = fer Gott! Hei = lig ift un = fer Gott!

BOTH CHOIRS.

Ho - ly art thou, our God, the Lord of Sa - ba - oth!
Hei = lig ift un = fer Gott, der Herr = re Ze = ba = oth!

FIRST CHOIR. **SECOND CHOIR.**

Thy maj - es - ty and god - ly might Fill the earth and all the realms of light.
Dein' gött = lich' Macht und Herr = lich = feit Gebt ü = ber Him = mel und Er = den weit.

The twelve a - pos - tles join in song With the dear proph-ets' good - ly throng.
The mar - tyrs' no - ble ar - my raise Their voice to thee in hymns of praise.
The u - ni - ver - sal Church doth thee Through-out the world con - fess to be
Der bei = li = gen zwölf Bo = ten Zahl, Und die lie = ben Pro = phe = ten all',
Die theu = ren Mär=t'rer all = zu = mal Lo = ben dich, Herr, mit gro = ßem Schall.
Die gan = ze wer = the Chri = sten = heit Rühmt dich auf Er = den al = le Zeit,

FIRST CHOIR. SECOND CHOIR.

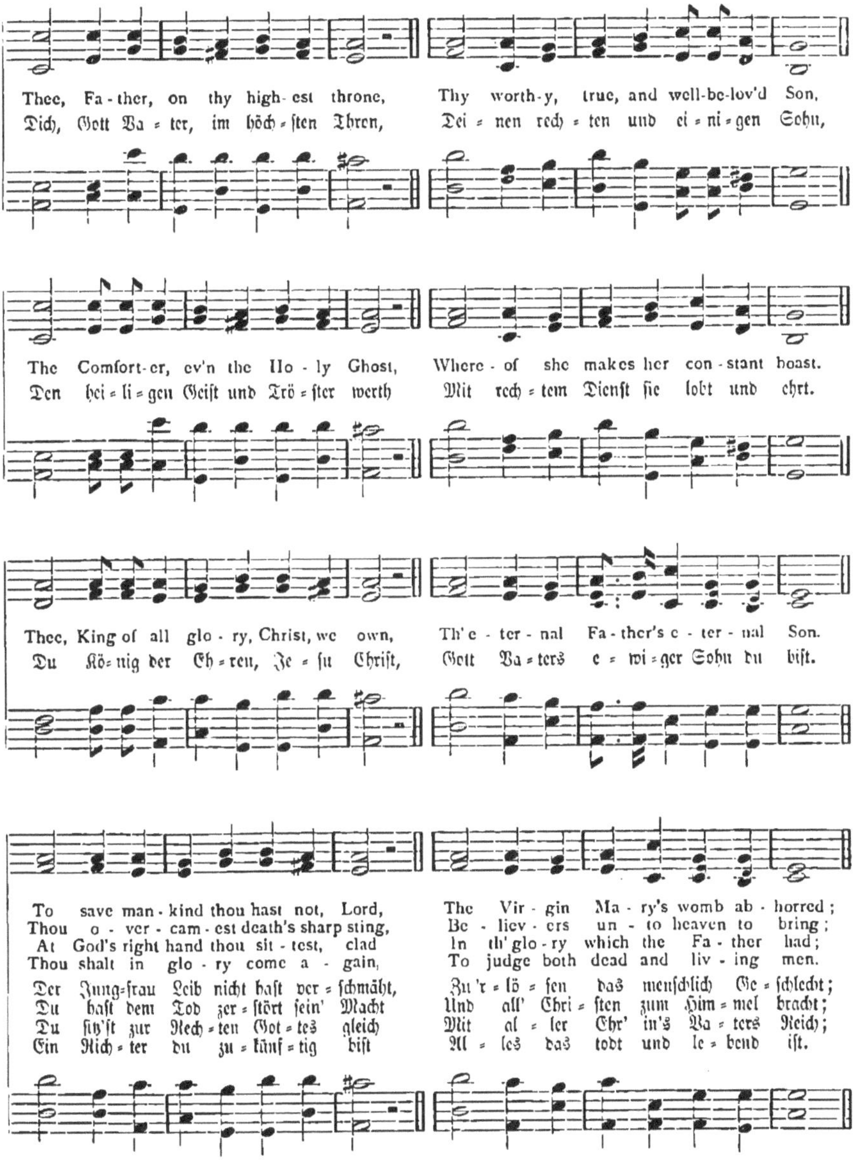

FIRST CHOIR.   **SECOND CHOIR.**

Thy serv-ants help whom thou, O   God,
Nun hilf uns, Herr, den Dieʒnern   dein,

Hast ransomed with that pre - ci-ous blood;
Die mit bei'm theu'rn Blut er = lö = set sein:

Grant that we share the heav'nly   rest
Laß uns im Him = mel ha = ben Theil

With the hap - py saints e - ter - nal-ly   blest.
Mit den Hei = li = gen in e = wigem Heil.

Help us, O Lord, from age to   age,
Hilf dei = nem Volk, Herr Je = su Christ,

And bless thy chos - en her - it - age.
Und seg = ne das dein Erb = theil ist;

Nour - ish and keep them by thy   power,
Wart' und pfleg' ihr'r zu al = ler Zeit

And lift them up for ev - er - more.
Und heb' sie hoch in E = wig = keit.

FIRST CHOIR.   **SECOND CHOIR.**

Lord God, we praise thee day by day,   And sanc - ti - fy thy name al - way.
Täg = lich, Herr Gott, wir lo = ben dich,   Und ehr'n dein Na = men ste = tig = lich.

.Keep us this day, and at all times,   From se - cret sins and o - pen crimes;
For mer - cy on - ly, Lord, we plead;   Be mer - ci - ful to our great need,
Show us thy mer - cy, Lord, as we   Our stead - fast trust re - pose in thee.
Be = hüt' uns heut', o treu = er Gott,   Für al = ler Sünd' und Miss = je = that,
Sei uns gnä = dig, o Her = re Gott,   Sei uns gnä = dig in al = ler Noth;
Zeig' uns dei = ne Barm=her = zig = keit,   Wie un = fre Hoff=nung zu dir steht.

In thee, Lord, have we put our trust;   O nev - er let our hope be lost!
Auf dich hof = fen wir, lie = ber Herr;   In Schan = den lass uns nim = mer = mehr!

BOTH CHOIRS.

A - - - - - - - - - men,..........................
A = = = = = = men,..........................

XXIX. Vom Himmel hoch da komm ich her.

From Heaven above to Earth I come.

A Christmas Song. LUKE, ii.

Melody, 1543.

From heav'n a - bove to earth I come, To bear good news to ev - 'ry home;

Glad ti - dings of great joy I bring, Where - of I now will say and sing.

1 Vom Himmel hoch da komm ich her,
Ich bring' euch gute neue Mähr,
Der guten Mähr bring ich so viel,
Davon ich sing'n und sagen will.

2 Euch ist ein Kindlein heut' gebor'n
Von einer Jungfrau auserkor'n,
Ein Kindelein so zart und fein,
Das soll eu'r Freud und Wonne sein.

3 Es ist der Herr Christ unser Gott,
Der will euch führ'n aus aller Noth,
Er will eu'r Heiland selber sein,
Von allen Sünden machen rein.

4 Er bringt euch alle Seligkeit,
Die Gott der Vater hat bereit't,
Daß ihr mit uns im Himmelreich
Sollt leben nun und ewiglich.

5 So merket nun das Zeichen recht,
Die Krippen, Windelein so schlecht,
Da findet ihr das Kind gelegt,
Das alle Welt erhält und trägt.

1 From heaven above to earth I come,
To bear good news to every home ;
Glad tidings of great joy I bring,
Whereof I now will say and sing.

2 To you, this night, is born a child
Of Mary, chosen Mother mild ;
This tender child of lowly birth,
Shall be the joy of all your earth.

3 'Tis Christ our God, who far on high
Had heard your sad and bitter cry ;
Himself will your salvation be,
Himself from sin will make you free.

4 He brings those blessings long ago
Prepared by God for all below ;
That in his heavenly kingdom blest
You may with us forever rest.

5 These are the tokens ye shall mark,
The swaddling-clothes and manger dark ;
There shall ye find the young child laid,
By whom the heavens and earth were made.

6 Deß laßt uns Alle fröhlich sein
Und mit den Hirten geh'n hinein,
Zu seh'n was Gott uns hat bescheert,
Mit seinem lieben Sohn verehrt.

7 Merk auf, mein Herz, und sieh dort hin:
Was liegt doch in dem Krippelein?
Weß ist das schöne Kindelein?
Es ist das liebe Jesulein.

8 Bis willekomm, du edler Gast,
Den Sünder nicht verschmähet hast,
Und kömmst in Elend her zu mir,
Wie soll ich immer danken dir?

9 Ach Herr, du Schöpfer aller Ding',
Wie bist du worden so gering,
Daß du da liegst auf dürrem Gras,
Davon ein Rind und Esel aß.

10 Und wär' die Welt vielmal so weit,
Von Edelstein und Gold bereit't,
So wär sie doch dir viel zu klein,
Zu sein ein enges Wiegelein.

11 Der Sammet und die Seiden dein,
Das ist grob Heu und Windelein,
Darauf du Kön'g so groß und reich
Herprangst, als wärs dein Himmelreich.

12 Das hat also gefallen dir,
Die Wahrheit anzuzeigen mir:
Wie aller Welt Macht, Ehr und Gut
Für dir nichts gilt, nichts hilft noch thut.

13 Ach, mein herzliebes Jesulein,
Mach dir ein rein sanft Bettelein,
Zu ruhen in mein's Herzens Schrein,
Daß ich nimmer vergesse dein.

14 Davon ich allzeit fröhlich sei,
Zu springen, singen immer frei
Das rechte Susanninne* schön, -
Mit Herzen Lust den süßen Ton.

15 Lob, Ehr sei Gott im höchsten Thron,
Der uns schenkt seinen ein'gen Sohn,
Des freuen sich der Engel Schaar
Und singen uns solch's neues Jahr.

* d. h. Wiegenliedlein.

6 Now let us all, with gladsome cheer,
Follow the shepherds, and draw near
To see this wondrous gift of God,
Who hath his own dear Son bestowed.

7 Give heed, my heart, lift up thine eyes!
What is it in yon manger lies?
Who is this child, so young and fair?
The blessed Christ-child lieth there!

8 Welcome to earth, thou noble guest,
Through whom e'en wicked men are blest!
Thou com'st to share our misery,
What can we render, Lord, to thee!

9 Ah, Lord, who hast created all,
How hast thou made thee weak and small,
To lie upon the coarse dry grass,
The food of humble ox and ass.

10 And were the world ten times as wide,
With gold and jewels beautified,
It would be far too small to be
A little cradle, Lord, for thee.

11 Thy silk and velvet are coarse hay,
Thy swaddling bands the mean array,
With which even thou, a King so great,
Art clad as with a robe of state.

12 Thus hath it pleased thee to make plain
The truth to us, poor fools and vain,
That this world's honor, wealth and might
Are naught and worthless in thy sight.

13 Ah, dearest Jesus, holy child,
Make thee a bed, soft, undefiled,
Here in my poor heart's inmost shrine,
That I may evermore be thine.

14 My heart for very joy doth leap,
My lips no more can silence keep,
I too must sing, with joyful tongue,
That sweetest ancient cradle song :—

15 Glory to God in highest heaven,
Who unto man his Son hath given,
While angels sing, with pious mirth,
A glad New Year to all the earth.

XXX. Sie ist mir lieb, die werthe Magd.

Dear is to me the holy Maid.

Founded on the twelfth chapter of the Revelation.

Melody, Wittenberg, 1545.   *Harmony by* M. PRAETORIUS, 1610.

Dear is to me the ho — — — — — — ly Maid,...... I
For glo-rious things of her .... are said ;...... Than

nev - er can for - get.. her ;
life I love her bet — — — — — — — [OMIT] ter : So dear and good,

That if I should Af - flict - ed be, It moves not me ; For she my soul will

rav — — — — — — ish With con - stan - cy and love's pure fire, And with her boun - ty   lav - - - ish   Ful - fill.............. my heart's de - sire

1 Sie ist mir lieb, die werthe Magd,
   Und kann ihr'r nicht vergessen,
Lob', Ehr' und Zucht von ihr man sagt,
   Sie hat mein Herz besessen.
     Ich bin ihr hold,
     Und wenn ich sollt
     Groß Unglück han,
     Da liegt nichts an;
   Sie will mich des ergötzen
Mit ihrer Lieb' und Treu an mir,
Die sie zu mir will setzen,
   Und thun all mein Begier.

2 Sie trägt von Gold so rein ein' Kron
   Da leuchten ihn zwölf Sterne,
Ihr Kleid ist wie die Sonne schön
   Das glänzet hell und ferne,
     Und auf dem Mon'
     Ihr' Füße ston
     Sie ist die Braut,
     Dem Herrn vertraut,
   Ihr ist weh, und muß g'bären
Ein schönes Kind, den edlen Sohn,
Und aller Welt ein'n Herren,
   Dem sie ist unterthon.

3 Das thut dem alten Drachen Zorn
   Und will das Kind verschlingen;
Sein Toben ist doch ganz verlor'n,
   Es kann ihm nicht gelingen:
     Das Kind ist doch
     Gen Himmel hoch
     Genommen hin,
     Und lässet ihn
   Auf Erden fast sehr wüthen;
Die Mutter muß gar sein allein,
Doch will sie Gott behüten,
   Und der recht' Vater sein.

1 Dear is to me the holy Maid,—
   I never can forget her;
For glorious things of her are said ;
   Than life I love her better :
     So dear and good,
     That if I should
     Afflicted be,
     It moves not me ;
   For she my soul will ravish
With constancy and love's pure fire,
And with her bounty lavish
   Fulfil my heart's desire.

2 She wears a crown of purest gold,
   Twelve shining stars attend her ;
Her raiment, glorious to behold,
   Surpasses far in splendor
     The sun at noon ;
     Upon the moon
     She stands, the Bride
     Of him who died :
   Sore travail is upon her ;
She bringeth forth a noble Son
Whom all the world doth honor ;
   She bows before his throne.

3 Thereat the Dragon raged, and stood
   With open mouth before her ;
But vain was his attempt, for God
   His buckler broad threw o'er her.
     Up to his throne
     He caught his Son,
     But left the foe
     To rage below.
   The mother, sore afflicted,
Alone into the desert fled,
There by her God protected,
   By her true Father fed.

XXXI. Vater unser im Himmelreich.

Our Father, Thou in Heaven above.

"Das Vaterunser, kurtz und gut ausgelegt, und in gesangsweise gebracht, durch D. Martin Luther." *The Lord's Prayer, paraphrased.*

Melody, 1538. ?   Harmony by A. Haupt, 1869.

Our Fa-ther, thou in heav'n a-bove, Who bid-dest us to dwell in love, As breth-ren of one fam-i-ly, And cry for all we need to thee; Teach us to mean the words we say, And from the in-most heart to pray.

1 Vater unser im Himmelreich,
Der du uns alle heißest gleich
Brüder sein, und dich rufen an
Und willt das Beten von uns han:
Gieb daß nicht bet allein der Mund,
Hilf daß es geh von Herzens Grund.

2 Geheiligt werd der Name dein,
Dein Wort bei uns hilf halten rein,
Daß auch wir leben heiliglich,
Nach deinem Namen würdiglich.
Behüt uns, Herr, für falscher Lehr,
Das arm verführet Volk bekehr.

1 Our Father, thou in heaven above,
Who biddest us to dwell in love,
As brethren of one family,
And cry for all we need to thee ;
Teach us to mean the words we say,
And from the inmost heart to pray.

2 All hallowed be thy name, O Lord !
O let us firmly keep thy Word,
And lead, according to thy name,
A holy life, untouched by blame ;
Let no false teachings do us hurt,—
All poor deluded souls convert.

3 Es komm dein Reich zu dieser Zeit
Und dort hernach in Ewigkeit;
Der heilig Geist uns wohne bei,
Mit seinen Gaben mancherlei;
Des Satans Zorn und groß Gewalt
Zerbrich, für ihm dein' Kirch' erhalt.

4 Dein Will gescheh', Herr Gott, zugleich
Auf Erden wie im Himmelreich,
Gib uns Geduld in Leidenszeit,
Gehorsam sein in Lieb und Leid,
Wehr und steu'r allem Fleisch und Blut,
Das wider deinen Willen thut.

5 Gib uns heut unser täglich Brot
Und was man darf zur Leibes Noth;
Behüt uns, Herr, für Unfried, Streit,
Für Seuchen und für theuer Zeit,
Daß wir in gutem Frieden stehn
Der Sorg und Geizens müßig gehen.

6 All unser Schuld' vergib uns, Herr,
Daß sie uns nicht betrüben mehr,
Wie wir auch unsern Schuldigern
Ihr Schuld und Fehl vergeben gern;
Zu dienen mach uns all bereit
In rechter Lieb und Einigkeit.

7 Führ uns, Herr, in Versuchung nicht,
Wenn uns der böse Feind anficht
Zur linken und zur rechten Hand,
Hilf uns thun starken Widerstand;
Im Glauben fest und wohlgerüst't
Und durch des heil'gen Geistes Trost.

8 Von allem Uebel uns erlös,
Es sind die Zeit und Tage bös;
Erlös uns vom ewigen Tod
Und tröst uns in der letzten Noth.
Bescher uns auch ein selig's End,
Nimm unser Seel in deine Händ'.

9 Amen, das ist: es werde wahr;
Stärk unsern Glauben immerdar,
Auf daß wir ja nicht zweifeln dran,
Daß wir hiermit gebeten han;
Auf dein Wort in dem Namen dein,
So sprechen wir das Amen fein.

3 Thy kingdom come ! Thine let it be
In time, and through eternity !
O let thy Holy Spirit dwell
With us, to rule and guide us well ;
From Satan's mighty power and rage
Preserve thy Church from age to age.

4 Thy will be done on earth, O Lord,
As where in heaven thou art adored !
Patience in time of grief bestow,
Thee to obey through weal and woe ;
Our sinful flesh and blood control
That thwart thy will within the soul.

5 Give us this day our daily bread,
Let us be duly clothed and fed,
And keep thou from our homes afar
Famine and pestilence and war,
That we may live in godly peace,
Unvexed by cares and avarice.

6 Forgive our sins, O Lord, that they
No more may vex us, day by day,
As we forgive their trespasses
Who unto us have done amiss ;
Thus let us dwell in charity,
And serve each other willingly.

7 Into temptation lead us not ;
And when the foe doth war and plot
Against our souls on every hand,
Then, armed with faith, O may we stand
Against him as a valiant host,
Through comfort of the Holy Ghost.

8 Deliver us from evil, Lord !
The days are dark and foes abroad ;
Redeem us from eternal death ;
And when we yield our dying breath,
Console us, grant us calm release,
And take our souls to thee in peace.

9 Amen ! that is, So let it be !
Strengthen our faith and trust in thee,
That we may doubt not, but believe
That what we ask we shall receive ;
Thus in thy name and at thy word
We say Amen, now hear us, Lord !

XXXII. Von Himmel kam der Engel Schaar.

To Shepherds, as they watched by Night.

A second Christmas Song, to the Tune, " Vom Himmel hoch."

Melody, 1543.

To shep-herds, as they watched by night, Ap-peared a troop of an-gels bright;

Be-hold the ten-der babe, they said, In yon-der low-ly man-ger laid.

1 Von Himmel kam der Engelschaar,
Erschien den Hirten offenbar;
Sie sagten ihn: Ein Kindlein zart
Das liegt dort in der Krippen hart.

2 Zu Bethlehem in Davids Statt,
Wie Micha das verkündet hat,
Es ist der Herre Jesus Christ
Der euer aller Heiland ist.

3 Des sollt ihr billig fröhlich sein,
Daß Gott mit euch ist worden ein;
Er ist gebor'n eu'r Fleisch und Blut,
Eu'r Bruder ist das ewig Gut.

4 Was kann euch thun die Sünd' und Tod?
Ihr habt mit euch den wahren Gott.
Laßt zürnen Teufel und die Höll'
Gott's Sohn ist 'worden eu'r Gesell.

5 Er will und kann euch lassen nicht,
Setzt ihr auf ihn eu'r Zuversicht;
Es mögen euch viel fechten an
Dem sei Trotz, der's nicht lassen kann.

1 To shepherds, as they watched by night,
Appeared a troop of angels bright;
Behold the tender babe, they said,
In yonder lowly manger laid.

2 At Bethlehem, in David's town,
As Micah did of old make known;—
'Tis Jesus Christ, your Lord and King,
Who doth to all salvation bring.

3 Rejoice ye, then, that through his Son
God is with sinners now at one;
Made like yourselves of flesh and blood,
Your brother is th' eternal Good.

4 What harm can sin and death then do?
The true God now abides with you:
Let hell and Satan chide and chafe,
God is your fellow—ye are safe.

5 Not one he will nor can forsake
Who him his confidence doth make:
Let all his wiles the tempter try,
You may his utmost powers defy.

6 Zuleht muß ihr doch haben recht,
Ihr seid nun 'worden Gott's Geschlecht;
Deß danket Gott in Ewigkeit,
Geruldig, fröhlich, alle Zeit.

6 You must prevail at last, for ye
Are now become God's family:
To God forever give ye praise,
Patient and cheerful all your days.

XXXIII. Erhalt uns, Herr, bei deinem Wort.

Lord, keep us in Thy Word and Work.

A Children's Song against the two arch-enemies of Christ and his Holy Church.

Melody, 1543.   *Harmony by* WM. STERNDALE BENNETT, 1865.

Lord, keep us in thy word and work, Re-strain the murderous Pope and Turk, Who

fain would tear from off thy throne, Christ Je - sus, thy be - lov - ed Son.

1 Erhalt' uns, Herr, bei deinem Wort
Und steure deine Feinde Mord,
Die Jesum Christum deinen Sohn,
Wollen stürzen von deinem Thron.

2 Beweis' dein Macht, Herr Jesu Christ,
Der du Herr allen Herren bist;
Beschirm' dein' arme Christenheit,
Daß sie dich lob' in Ewigkeit.

3 Gott heil'ger Geist, du Tröster werth,
Gieb' dei'm Volk ein'rlei Sinn' auf Erd'
Steh bei uns in der letzten Noth,
G'leit uns ins Leben aus dem Tod.

1 Lord, keep us in thy word and work,
Restrain the murderous Pope and Turk,
Who fain would tear from off thy throne
Christ Jesus, thy belovéd Son.

2 Lord Jesus Christ, thy power make known,
For thou art Lord of lords alone.
Shield thy poor Christendom, that we
May evermore sing praise to thee.

3 God, Holy Ghost, our joy thou art,
Give to thy flock on earth one heart.
Stand by us in our latest need,
And us from death to glory lead.

NOTE.—To these three stanzas by Luther, three more have been added by a later hand.

XXXIV. Christ, unser Herr, zum Jordan kam.

To Jordan came our Lord the Christ.

This melody, known also by the title, " Es soll uns Gott genädig sein," is supposed to have been taken from a secular tune of much earlier date.

Harmony by A. HAUPT, 1869.

{ To Jor - dan came our Lord the Christ, To do God's pleas - ure will - ing, }
{ And there was by Saint John bap - tized, All right - eous - ness ful - fil - ing ; } There

did he con - se - crate a bath To wash a - way trans - gres - sion, And quench the bit - ter-

ness of death By his own blood and pas - sion ; He would a new life give.... us.

1 Christ, unser Herr, zum Jordan kam
   Nach seines Vaters Willen,
Von Sanct Johann's die Taufe nahm,
   Sein Werk und Amt zu 'rfüllen.
Da wollt' er stiften uns ein Bad,
   Zu waschen uns von Sünden,
Ersäufen auch den bittern Tod
   Durch sein selbst Blut und Wunden,
     Es galt ein neues Leben.

2 So hört und merket alle wohl,
   Was Gott heißt selbst die Taufe,
Und was ein Christen glauben soll,
   Zu meiden Ketzer Haufen:
Gott spricht und will, das Wasser sei
   Doch nicht allein schlecht Wasser,
Sein heilig's Wort ist auch dabei
   Mit reichem Geist ohn' Maßen,
     Der ist allhie der Täufer.

1 To Jordan came our Lord the Christ,
   To do God's pleasure willing,
And there was by Saint John baptized,
   All righteousness fulfilling ;
There did he consecrate a bath
   To wash away transgression,
And quench the bitterness of death
   By his own blood and passion ;
     He would a new life give us.

2 So hear ye all, and well perceive
   What God doth call baptism,
And what a Christian should believe
   Who error shuns and schism :
That we should water use, the Lord
   Declareth it his pleasure ;
Not simple water, but the Word
   And Spirit without measure ;
     He is the true Baptizer.

3 Solch's hat er uns beweiset klar,
Mit Bildern und mit Worten,
Des Vaters Stimm man offenbar
Daselbst am Jordan hörte.
Er sprach: das ist mein lieber Sohn,
An dem ich hab' Gefallen,
Den will ich euch befohlen han,
Daß ihr ihn höret alle
Und folget seinen Lehren.

4 Auch Gottes Sohn hie selber steht
In seiner zarten Menschheit,
Der heilig' Geist hernieder fährt
In Taubenbild verkleidet;
Daß wir nicht sollen zweifeln d'ran,
Wenn wir getaufet werden,
All' drei Person getaufet han,
Damit bei uns auf Erden
Zu wohnen sich ergeben.

5 Sein' Jünger heißt der Herre Christ:
Geht hin all' Welt zu lehren,
Daß sie verlor'n in Sünden ist,
Sich soll zur Buße kehren;
Wer glaubet und sich taufen läßt,
Soll daturch selig werden,
Ein neugeborner Mensch er heißt,
Der nicht mehr könne sterben,
Das Himmelreich soll erben,

6 Wer nicht glaubt dieser großen G'nad,
Der bleibt in seinen Sünden,
Und ist verdammt zum ew'gen Tod
Tief in der Höllen Grunde,
Nichts hilft sein' eigen' Heiligkeit,
All' sein Thun ist verloren.
Die Erbsünd' macht's zur Nichtigkeit,
Darin er ist geboren,
Vermag ihm selbst nichts helfen.

7 Das Aug' allein das Wasser sieht,
Wie Menschen Wasser gießen,
Der Glaub' im Geist die Kraft versteht
Des Blutes Jesu Christi,
Und ist für ihm ein' rothe Fluth
Von Christus Blut gefärbet,
Die allen Schaden heilen thut
Von Adam her geerbet,
Auch von uns selbst begangen.

3 To show us this, he hath his word
With signs and symbols given;
On Jordan's banks was plainly heard
The Father's voice from heaven:
"This is my well-belovéd Son,
In whom my soul delighteth;
Hear him." Yea, hear him every one
Whom he himself inviteth,
Hear and obey his teaching.

4 In tender manhood Jesus straight
To holy Jordan wendeth;
The Holy Ghost from heaven's gate
In dovelike shape descendeth;
That thus the truth be not denied,
Nor should our faith e'er waver,
That the Three Persons all preside
At Baptism's holy laver,
And dwell with the believer.

5 Thus Jesus his disciples sent:
Go, teach ye every nation,
That lost in sin they must repent,
And flee from condemnation:
He that believes and is baptized,
Obtains a mighty blessing;
A new-born man, no more he dies,
Eternal life possessing,
A joyful heir of heaven.

6 Who in this mercy hath not faith,
Nor aught therein discerneth,
Is yet in sin, condemned to death,
And fire that ever burneth;
His holiness avails him not,
Nor aught which he is doing;
His inborn sin brings all to naught,
And maketh sure his ruin;
Himself he cannot succor.

7 The eye of sense alone is dim,
And nothing sees but water;
Faith sees Christ Jesus, and in him
The lamb ordained for slaughter;
She sees the cleansing fountain red
With the dear blood of Jesus,
Which from the sins inherited
From fallen Adam frees us,
And from our own misdoings.

70

XXXV. Was fürcht'st du, Feind Herodus, sehr?

Why, Herod, unrelenting Foe.

From the Hymn of Cœlius Sedelius, of the Fifth Century, " Herodes hostis impie."

Harmony by M. Praetorius, 1609.

Why, He-rod, un-re-lent-ing foe, Doth the Lord's com-ing move thee so? He

doth no earth-ly king-dom seek, Who brings his king-dom to...... the meek.

1 Was fürcht'st du, Feind Herodes, sehr,
Daß uns gebor'n kommt Christ der Herr?
Er sucht kein sterblich Königreich,
Der zu uns bringt sein Himmelreich.

2 Dem Stern die Weisen folgen nach,
Solch' Licht zum rechten Licht sie bracht';
Sie zeigen mit den Gaben drei,
Dies Kind, Gott, Mensch, und König sei.

3 Die Tauf' im Jordan an sich nahm
Das himmelische Gottes Lamm,
Dadurch, der nie kein' Sünde that,
Von Sünden uns gewaschen hat.

4 Ein Wunderwerk da neu geschah;
Sechs steinern' Krüge man da sah
Voll Wasser, das verlor sein Art,
Rother Wein durch sein Wort d'raus ward.

5 Lob, Ehr' und Dank sei dir gesagt,
Christ, gebor'n von der reinen Magd,
Mit Vater und dem heiligen Geist
Von nun an bis in Ewigkeit.

1 Why, Herod, unrelenting foe,
Doth the Lord's coming move thee so?
He doth no earthly kingdom seek
Who brings his kingdom to the meek.

2 Led by the star, the wise men find
The Light that lightens all mankind;
The threefold presents which they bring
Declare him God, and Man, and King.

3 In Jordan's sacred waters stood
The meek and heavenly Lamb of God,
And he who did no sin, thereby
Cleansed us from all iniquity!

4 And now a miracle was done:
Six waterpots stood there of stone;
Christ spake the word with power divine,
The water reddened into wine.

5 All honor unto Christ be paid,
Pure offspring of the holy maid,
With Father and with Holy Ghost,
Till time in endless time be lost.

XXXVI. Der du bist Drei in Einigkeit.

Thou, who art Three in Unity.

An imitation from the Gregorian hymn, " O lux beata trinitas."

Original Latin Melody.　　　　　　　　　　　　*Harmony in* VON TUCHER, 18—.

Thou who art Three in U - ni - ty,　True God from all e - ter - ni - ty,

The sun is fad - ing from our sight,　Shine thou on us with heav'n - ly light.

1 Der du bist drei in Einigkeit,
　Ein wahrer Gott von Ewigkeit;
　Die Sonn' mit dem Tag von uns weicht:
　Laß leuchten uns dein göttlich Licht.

2 Des Morgens, Gott, dich loben wir,
　Des Abends auch beten für dir,
　Unser armes Lied rühmt dich
　Jetzt und immer und ewiglich.

3 Gott Vater, dem sei ewig Ehr,
　Gott Sohn der ist der einig' Herr,
　Und dem Tröster heiligen Geist,
　Von nun an bis in Ewigkeit.

1 Thou who art Three in Unity,
　True God from all eternity,
　The sun is fading from our sight,
　Shine thou on us with heavenly light.

2 We praise thee with the dawning day,
　To thee at evening also pray,
　With our poor song we worship thee
　Now, ever and eternally.

3 Let God the Father be adored,
　And God the Son, the only Lord,
　And equal adoration be,
　Eternal Comforter, to thee.